Waitman Thomas Willey

A Sketch of the Life of Philip Doddridge

Waitman Thomas Willey

A Sketch of the Life of Philip Doddridge

ISBN/EAN: 9783337416874

Printed in Europe, USA, Canada, Australia, Japan

Cover: Foto ©Thomas Meinert / pixelio.de

More available books at **www.hansebooks.com**

A SKETCH

OF

THE LIFE

OF

PHILIP DODDRIDGE.

BY

W. T. WILLEY.

READ BEFORE THE WEST VIRGINIA HISTORICAL SOCIETY,
AT ITS ANNUAL MEETING HELD IN THE
WEST VIRGINIA UNIVERSITY,
JUNE, 1875.

PUBLISHED BY ORDER OF THE SOCIETY.

MORGANTOWN:
MORGAN & HOFFMAN, PRINTERS.
1875.

PREFATORY.

In the preparation of the following sketch, the same disappointment has been encountered which often presents itself to the biographer of persons of even the greatest distinction—the meagerness of personal details and private history, that can be satisfactorily authenticated after the lapse of a generation from the time of their decease. Indeed, it is not an unfrequent fact, that men of the highest order of intellect, and who have participated largely, and influentially, in the various learned professions, have, nevertheless, left few and inadequate proofs of their great talents and activities. This is especially so, in the case of those who have been chiefly distinguished as members of the Bar. The judge on the Bench leaves the evidences of his learning and ability in his recorded decisions; the philosopher is known by his discoveries; the poet by his works; the historian by his annals; and the statesman by his measures of public policy incorporated in the legislation of his country. But in respect of the most eminent of them, there are many instances, where we can ascertain but little of their personal habits, private life, and social characteristics.

No scholar, or man of taste, will acknowledge himself to be unacquainted with The Iliad and Odyssey; yet, nothing is known of their author, excepting his name; and even that is disputed by some. How meager is the personal history of Shakespeare! The fame of many a genius is merely traditional. Our own Patrick Henry, for instance. If we were to judge of his oratory, only by the examples he has left, he would hardly be entitled to the merit of mediocrity. No faithful pen was present with the living orator to transfer his wonderful eloquence to the enduring page; and the witnesses of it, passed away with his co-temporaries. So it has been with many of our eminent barristers and advocates. Their learning, eloquence and intellectual achievements, exerted in the judicial forum, have left no memorial, but the naked verdicts of juries, and formal decrees of courts, which are silent as to the forensic power and ability which secured them. Doubtless, the judicial opinions of the bench shine, oftentimes, with a lustre borrowed from the light shed upon the questions adjudicated, by the counsel who discussed them at the bar; but the barrister receives no credit for it. This, however, is no unusual thing. Many a reaper gathers a rich harvest where he never sowed; and there are those in every sphere of life, who enjoy the credit of merit justly due to others. It has often happened, in the history of the world, that the greatest events were, primarily, assignable to agencies unacknowledged and unrecognized in the processes of their accomplishment. Revolutions, changing the aspect and

conditions of nations, not unfrequently have their sources
in the quiet study of the philosopher, who, from the depths
of his own mind and heart, silently evolves those original
principles and moral forces, which set the world in motion;
and the visible actors, like the index hands on the face of a
watch, moved around by the hidden power of the invisible
mainspring, unconsciously mark the progress of mankind
on "the dial-plate of time." Yet it is these external agents,
who make history. They receive the renown. They become famous. Their deeds are chronicled; whilst the poor
intellectual factor who pointed out the way to glory, seldom
finds a biographer; and when he does, his life is so barren
of incident, and stirring adventure, as to secure, only here
and there, a reader, who likes to trace effects back to their
causes, and who is willing to accord to moral and intellectual excellence, a paramount consideration.

The true life of the eminent barrister and advocate, can
never be written. His co-temporaries might have described
his public efforts, if they had been present to witness them.
But his greatest achievements are not wrought in public.
They are accomplished when there are no witnesses, alone,
in his office, among his books and his briefs. There he
organizes his victories; there he detects the fraud; there
he discovers the guilt; there he equips himself for the vindication of justice; there he foils the devices of the treach-
erous adversary; there, from all the history, and philosophy,
and jurisprudence of the past, he qualifies himself for the
discharge of the duties of a profession, which, in the lan-

guage of Dr. Johnson, "requires the greatest powers of the
mind applied to the greatest number of purposes."

The subject of this sketch has been dead forty-two years.
Much the larger portion of his mature life had been exclusively devoted to the practice of the law. Only one of his
legal arguments, so far as is now known, was ever published;
and that was made in the House of Representatives of the
United States, near the close of his life. The consequence
is, that this period of his career, furnishes little of either
professional or private history, excepting what is traditional.

BIRTH, EDUCATION, MARRIAGE, &C.

PHILIP DODDRIDGE, the subject of this sketch, was the second son of John Doddridge, who was a native of Maryland, born there in the year 1745, where, on the 22nd December, 1765, he married Mary, the daughter of Richard Wells, of that State. They emigrated from Maryland to Bedford county, Pennsylvania; and there, Philip was born on the 17th of May, 1772. In the Spring of 1773, they removed to Washington county, Pennsylvania. There is still standing, near Middletown in that county, an old church, known as the "Doddridge Chapel," on the farm where John Doddridge then settled, and where he continued to reside until he died in April, 1791. It was built by himself for the use of the Methodist Episcopal Church; and it is said to have been the first chapel erected for that denomination west of the Allegheny mountains.

At that time, this place was within the jurisdiction, and was supposed to be in the territory, of Virginia. But afterwards, when Mason and Dixon's line was established, and the western boundary of Pennsylvania was drawn due north from the western terminus of Mason and Dixon's line, the residence of the Doddridge family was included, by a short distance, within the territory of Pennsylvania.

The writer has been furnished with what purports to be

"an extract from the records of the Doddridge family," in which it is alleged that "John Doddridge, was the son of Joseph and Mary Doddridge." There is reason to doubt the correctness of this statement. There still remains in the possession of a niece of the subject of this sketch, (Mrs. Polsley, wife of Hon. Daniel Polsley, of Point Pleasant, West Virginia,) an old book—"Hall's Meditations"—printed in London in 1617, which appears to have been a kind of *heir-loom* in the family. On the title page of this book, there is a memorandum in the handwriting of John Doddridge, as follows:

"*Once the property of John Charldton, of Fredericktown, Maryland. After his decease, the property of Joseph Doddridge, of the same place. After his decease, it became the property of Philip Doddridge, son of Joseph Doddridge. Written by me, Jan. 1st, in the year of our Lord, one thousand seven hundred and eighty-seven.*   JOHN DODDRIDGE.*"

Judge Polsley, to whom we are indebted for this transscript, adds: "This John Doddridge, although he does not say so, was the son of the *elder* Philip, and the father of *our* Philip." It is possible, however, that this John Doddridge, although he does not say so, may have had a brother named Philip, who was the last named proprietor of the book.

The first ancestor of the family in this country, came from England, and settled in the colony of New Jersey. He was of the same stock as the celebrated Philip Doddridge, author of "The Rise and Progress of Religion in the Soul;" and was said to have been nearly related to him.

During the minority of young Philip, the facilities for acquiring an education, were very meagre, in the vicinity of his place of residence. There were neither colleges, nor academies there; and the common schools were of an inferior character. Indeed, there were few schools of any grade. Nor did the circumstances of his parents, enable them to send him to distant seats of learning. Until he was seventeen years of age, he was kept at home, working upon the farm; receiving, however, from his father, who was a "good English scholar," such instruction, as the intervals of their toil permitted the one to give, and the other to receive. At the age of seventeen, he was placed at school, in Charlestown (now Wellsburg, Brooke county, West Virginia,) under the tuition of a gentleman by the name of Johnson. Here he remained a short time, devoting himself, principally, to the study of the latin language.

A writer* in the *American Pioneer*, shortly after the death of Mr. Doddridge, says:

"His vigorous mind drank in knowledge with the rapidity of thought, as a dry sponge absorbs water. It soon became a habit with him, to exercise his memory in changing the conversation around him into the idiom of his studies; and following his father in his evening and morning devotions, he soon learned to render his prayers into very good latin, and to converse with his teacher fluently. This close application to his books, although it invigorated his mental powers, yet enfeebled his body, and it became necessary, for awhile, to suspend his studies."

He had an elder brother, Joseph Doddridge, who, afterwards became an Episcopal Clergyman, and, also, was the author of an interesting book, entitled: "*Notes on the settlement and Indian Wars of the Western parts of Virginia and Pennsylvania, from the year* 1763 *until the year* 1783, *inclusive, together with a view of the state of society and manners of the first settlers of that country.*" The following extract from this work will show some of the difficulties and deprivations

* Dr. S. P. Hildreth.

which surrounded the earlier days of the subject of this
paper:

"The settlements on this side of the mountains commenced along the Mo-
nongahela river, and between that river and the Laurel Ridge, in the year
1772. In the succeeding year they reached the Ohio river.   *   *

*   *   *   *   *   *   *   *   *

"Some of the earlier settlers took the precaution to come over the mountains in the spring, leaving their families behind, to raise a crop of corn, and
then return and bring them out in the fall. This I should think was the
better way. Others, especially those whose families were small, brought
them with them in the spring. My father took the latter course. His family
was but small, and he brought them all with him. The Indian meal which
he brought over the mountain was expended six weeks too soon, so that for
that length of time, we had to live without bread. The lean venison, and
the breast of wild turkeys, we were taught to call bread. The flesh of the
bear was denominated meat. This artifice did not succeed very well. After
living in this way for some time, we became sickly, the stomach seemed to be
always empty and tormented with a sense of hunger. I remember how nar-
rowly the children watched the growth of the potato tops, pumpkin and
squash vines, hoping from day to day to get something to answer in the place
of bread. How delicious was the taste of the young potatoes when we got
them. What a jubilee when we were permitted to pull the young corn for
roasting ears. Still more so, when it had acquired sufficient hardness to be
made into Jonny-cakes by the aid of the tin grater. We then became healthy,
vigorous, and contented with our situation, poor as it was.

" My father, with a small number of his neighbors, made their settlements
in the spring of 1773. Though they were in a poor and destitute situation,
they, nevertheless, lived in peace ; but their tranquility was not of long con-
tinuance. Those most atrocious murders of the peaceable, inoffensive Indians
at Captina and Yellow Creek, brought on the war of Lord Dunmore in the
spring of 1774. Our little settlement then broke up. The women and children were removed to Morris's Fort, in Sandy Creek Glade, some distance to
the east of Uniontown. The fort consisted of an assemblage of small hovels,
situated on the margin of a large and noxious marsh, the effluvia of which
gave most of the women and children the fever and ague. The men were
compelled, by necessity, to return home, and risk the tomahawk and scalping
knife of the Indian, in raising corn to keep their families from starvation the

succeeding winter. Those sufferings, dangers, and losses, were the tribute we had to pay to that thirst for blood which actuated those veteran murderers who brought the war upon us."

It is not surprising, therefore, that growing up into manhood, in the midst of such disadvantages, dangers and difficulties, the early education of Mr. Doddridge was limited and imperfect—such as he would acquire from casual opportunities, and by his own unaided efforts, exerted amid the struggles for the means of subsistence.   That he made good proficiency, under the circumstances, may be inferred from the following amusing incident:

At this early day, the principal commercial relations of the district of country where he lived, bordering on the Ohio river, were with the town of New Orleans, then under the dominion of Spain.   The chief staples of trade from the section named, were flour and bacon, floated down the river in what were called "Kentucky," or "flat-bottomed boats." Young Doddridge, not yet arrived at his majority, curious to see something of the world, made an engagement with the proprietors of one of these boats to accompany them, partly in the character of a common laborer, and partly as supercargo, rendering such services in consideration of his passage, and support, during the voyage.   Whilst the boat had stopped at Natchez, where the Spanish governor then resided, the youthful traveler availed himself of the delay, to stroll about town, occasionally, to gratify his curiosity. During one of these rambles, he met the governor. Finding that neither of them understood the vernacular of the other, Doddridge addressed his Excellency in the Latin language, and was responded to in the same tongue.   Surprised, that one so young, and, withal, so coarsely clad, could converse in a dead language, the governor prolonged the interview—

his surprise being continually augmented by the sprightliness, intelligence, and general information of the uncouth lad. The result was an invitation to dine at the executive mansion, and other flattering attentions. When the highly honored guest returned to the boat, he was boisterously saluted by the wondering crew, who, in the rude dialect peculiar to their class and vocation, demanded of him to know what it was that the "old Spanish fool" could see in him worthy of such distinction. Young Doddridge facetiously replied that "It was all owing to his beauty." The point of this pleasantry consisted in the fact, that whilst he was, physically, strongly developed, he was by no means distinguished by the personal graces of an Adonis.

After his return from New Orleans, young Doddridge procured a few elementary law-books, such as Blackstone's Commentaries, Bacon's Abridgement, Coke upon Littleton, &c., and addressed himself to the study of the law for two or three years, with little or no assistance besides his own resolution, industry, and genius. Where he resided during his period of professional preparation, and for some years afterwards, we have no definite information; but on the 24th of December, 1829, he casually remarked in a debate in the constitutional convention of Virginia that: "He had resided within the district where his home now was, for thirty-three years." That home was Wellsburg, Brooke county; so that he must have settled there in 1796. And here he lived thenceforward until his decease.

In 1799 Mr. Doddridge married Miss Juliana P. Musser, of Lancaster Pennsylvania, who survived him twenty-seven years. She died at Liverpool, Fulton county, Illinois, in the year 1859.

The village thus selected by Mr. Doddridge as his place

of residence, is pleasantly situated on the east bank of the
Ohio river, about sixteen miles above the city of Wheeling.
The plateau, or bottom land on which it is located, is boun-
ded on the east by a parallel range of hills, rising gently
and gracefully to a considerable height, variegated with
forest and field.   On the opposite side of the river, the hills
of Ohio, more abrupt and irregular, but equally picturesque,
crowd down nearer to the margin of the stream.   It was a
quiet but charming place for a home.   Midway in the town
stood the mansion last occupied by Mr. Doddridge, quite on
the verge of the river.   From the porch extending back
from the main part of the dwelling, the river was visible for
a considerable distance above and below.   Here, toward
the latter part of his life, he delighted to sit in the balmy
air of a spring day, watching the passing steamboats, then
hardly ever out of sight, conversing with his friends, descri-
bing the progress of the country's improvement during the
previous quarter of a century, and patriotically predicting
the grander progress still to come.   Here too, in this seclu-
ded abode, cut off from those facilities of instruction and
information to which ordinary men are usually indebted for
whatsoever of eminence they achieve, were developed and
matured, those rare professional attainments and intellectual
powers, which were to become the admiration of the Bar,
the Bench, and the Legislative assembly.

AT THE BAR.

Having thus "established himself in life," as well as in the profession he had adopted, he pursued it with little intermission, until the autumn of 1829. There is, as has been already intimated, little in the routine of the life of a member of the Bar, to excite the public attention. The investigation of abstruse and naked questions of law before the courts, or the trial of issues of fact before juries, has seldom much attraction beyond the limited circle of those directly interested in the result. This was more especially so at that time, which was before the era of the modern Journalist and Reporter. Nevertheless his growing reputation, as an able counsellor and advocate, soon extended beyond the quiet village where he resided, until he became famous in most of the counties of North-western Virginia. The loose and improvident mode of seating, and of securing patents for, waste and unappropriated lands, authorized by the laws of Virginia, and the unskilful and imperfect manner of locating and surveying them, partly resulting from the ignorance of the surveyors employed, and partly from the dangerous presence of the Indians still lurking in the forests, when many of the surveys were made, had so confused and complicated the titles to lands in North-western Virginia, as that they became the fruitful subject of litigation of the most embarrassing character. Many of these tracts of land,

of large areas, fell into the hands of minor heirs, living in
Eastern Virginia, and others passed to non residents of the
State; and consequently they were frequently omitted from
the assessors' books; and often the taxes due thereon, were
not paid.   This state of affairs led to a system of legislation
imposing penalties for delinquencies for the non-payment
of taxes, forfeiture for non-entries, &c., of the most arbitrary,
artificial and technical character, resulting in still greater
complexity and confusion.   The clear, rapid, and compre-
hensive mind of Mr. Doddridge, was peculiarly fitted to
grapple with the difficult and diverse questions springing
out of these circumstances; and he was largely retained as
counsel in a majority of the counties North-west of the Al-
leghenies.   He came to be acknowledged as among the first,
if not the first lawyer in that section of the State.   His practice also extended into the State of Ohio, and into Western
Pennsylvania.

In the latter State, he frequently encountered at the bar,
those eminent lawyers, Baldwin, Ross, Kennedy, Campbell,
McGiffin, and others, of almost equal celebrity, who were
then in the meridian of their professional life.

The venerable Joseph Johnson, of Bridgeport, Harrison
county, West Virginia, late governor of Virginia, still "lingering on the shores of time," crowned with the honors of
a long and distinguished public life, in an interesting letter
recently addressed to the author, says:

"I became acquainted with Philip Doddridge about the year 1807, or 1808,
who was then a young lawyer attending court in the town of Clarksburg,
when he occupied a prominent position at the bar, and ranked among the
most eminent counsellors of Western Virginia.   Among the first political
discussions I ever listened to, was one between him and Gen. J. G. Jackson,
which occurred in Clarksburg during the canvass which preceded the election

of Madison to the Presidency of the United States. The former, belonged to what was called the Federal, and the other, to the Republican party. They were champions well chosen, and foemen worthy of each other's steel; and it was appropriately styled a meeting of the Greeks."

It was during the earlier part of his professional career, that a gentleman in western Pennsylvania, becoming involved in an important law-suit, found that his antagonist had secured the services of the principal lawyers in the vicinity. It, therefore, became necessary to look elsewhere for counsel of adequate ability to meet this array of professional talent. The gentleman went to Virginia and employed Mr. Doddridge to assist in the defence of his case. When the trial came on, Mr. Doddridge seemed much indisposed, resting his head on the table before him, and apparently slumbering, during the examination of the witnesses, and the opening argument of the plaintiff's counsel. His client was alarmed, and his adversary was elated. But when the proper time arrived, Mr. Doddridge, arousing himself from his seeming stupor, rose to reply; "when," in the language of our informant, "his accurate recollection of everything that had occurred, his clear statement of the facts and points in the case, his massive arguments, his logical conclusions, his citations of authorities, his summary of the evidence, and masterly exposition of the law, astonished the bench, the bar and the audience, reversed the scene, and secured a verdict for his client."

Another anecdote connected with his practice in western Pennsylvania, will illustrate his power and tact as an advocate.

A drover stopping at a tavern, was murdered and robbed. Circumstances pointed to the landlord, who had hitherto sustained an excellent character, as the party guilty of the

2

crime, and he was indicted for murder. An idler about the
premises, assumed the character of an accomplice and ac-
cessary, and proposed to turn State's evidence, and testify
that the landlord was the principal. The celebrated Ross,
of Pittsburgh, Parker Campbell, and Mr. Doddridge, were
employed in the defence,—an array of professional talent
not often united in the same cause. In addition to circumstances, which the accused was unable to explain, the testimony of this witness was explicit and positive as to his
guilt. Against these the accused could only present a reputation of hitherto unsullied probity of character. But the
circumstantial evidence, and the positive testimony of this
self-confessed accomplice, were so direct and clear, that
Ross and Campbell, had, apparently, made no satisfactory
impression upon the jury. Campbell so told Mr. Doddridge,
and appealed to him to come to the rescue. But Mr. Doddridge, leaning against the railing of the bar, in a rather
careless attitude, addressed the jury to the following effect:

"May it please your Honor—gentlemen of the jury! I am not about to
make a speech, but wish simply to relate a fact. Down in Eastern Virginia,
in my younger days, there lived a celebrated lawyer, by the name of Gabriel
Jones. He was of the old school of Virginia gentlemen."

Mr. Doddridge then described his cocked hat, his frilled
shirt-bosom and wristbands, his powdered hair, blue coat,
white vest and cravat, silk stockings, and silver knee and
shoe-buckles, so vividly, that if Mr. Gabriel Jones had been
standing at the bar of the court, the impression of his appearance on the minds of the jury, could not have been
more distinct and palpable:

"Well, gentlemen of the jury, when Fauquier county was set off, and held
its first court, Mr. Jones went up there to attend to his professional engage-
ments. He arrived on Sunday morning, where he found several junior mem-

bers of the bar, who, being desirous of shewing him such attentions as might be agreeable to him, invited him to go and hear a celebrated, but, somewhat eccentric preacher who was to occupy a pulpit in town that day. Arriving at the door, they stood aside for their honored senior to precede them. The preacher had commenced his discourse; and as Gabriel Jones walked in, he put his cocked hat under his arm, and reverently walked up the aisle. The preacher paused, and pointing his long finger toward him, exclaimed: 'Ah! you old sinner with your cocked hat under your arm; your hair not white enough, but you must powder it — you come into the house of God, after his services have commenced. I will appear as a witness against you in the day of judgment!' Jones looked his reprover calmly in the face, and said: 'I have no doubt you will, for in the course of a long practice, I have always found that the grandest rascal turned State's evidence.'"

It is impossible to transfer the manner of Mr. D. to the page; nor is it pretended that the foregoing sketch does justice to the style and language of the recital. But the effect was electric. The jury was not only diverted by the anecdote, but its influence on their judgment, in connection with the good character of the accused, bore down the testimony of the witness, secured an acquittal of the accused, and saved an innocent man from an ignominious death.

The physical toil of an extensive legal practice in North Western Virginia, during the period of Mr. Doddridge's earlier life, was of no small magnitude. The area of most of the counties was large; and, consequently, the seats of justice were far apart. The only practicable mode of traveling between them was on horseback, over rough, and sometimes, precipitous roads. Nevertheless, the superior courts were anticipated with pleasure by the members of the Bar. In many instances, there was but one tavern of tolerable pretensions at the county seat; and here, the *elite* of the profession, from the surrounding counties, formed pleasant re-unions at every returning term — furnishing opportunities of great social enjoyment, that resulted in a happy moral and intellectual influence on the profession. Often, after the adjournment of the court for the day, legal principles were discussed by the Bar; and whenever it was so, Mr. D., if present, was the oracle. If, as was most usually the case, conversation of a general character ensued, he was still the central figure of the group, charming the whole circle by his inexhaustible treasure of wisdom, wit and anecdote. Here and there, you may still find, lingering among us, an old member of the bar, who delights to recur to those memorable occasions.

He was sometimes retained in important cases in the Court of Appeals at Richmond, Virginia, involving the necessity of traveling three hundred miles, or more, in the saddle, across the Allegheny and Blue Ridge mountains. He was also called to the argument of cases in the Supreme Court of the United States. His presence there, in 1822, was noticed by Mr. Justice Story, in a letter to his wife, dated the 28th of February of that year. It refers to such a "curious circumstance," relating to Mr. D., that it can hardly be deemed inappropriate to allow a place for the following extract :

"A curious circumstance has been related to me at this term, respecting a gentleman now attending this court, which the melancholy associations of this time (the death of the celebrated Pinckney is referred to) have brought to my recollection. The person to whom I refer, is Mr. Doddridge, eminent for his talents at the Bar. * * * * * * About two months since, he was suddenly seized with an apoplexy, palsy, catalepsy, or some disease of that nature, and the powers of life seemed entirely suspended. The physicians declared him dead, and the persons in the house proceeded to lay out the corpse. During all this time he says he was perfectly in his senses, hearing all that was said, but was totally unable to move a muscle, or to make the slightest exertion. While these things were going on, his wife thought she perceived a slight motion in one of his legs, the knee being drawn up. She supposed it an involuntary muscular motion, and on placing the limb down, it was again slightly moved; she was struck by the circumstance, raised his head high upon a pillow, rubbed him with brandy, and soon perceived a slight indication of returning life. He slowly revived, and is here now arguing cases. He says that the motion of his knees was voluntary; aware of his situation and all its horrors, he was just able to make the slightest motion, and every time any one came near the bed, renewed it, until the motion was observed. This story is almost marvellous; but the gentleman has told it himself to one of the judges, and the story has been confirmed by other gentlemen well knowing the facts."*

It appears that Mr. D., fearing a recurrence of so perilous a mistake, had instructed his family and friends never to bury him, however apparent his death might be, until every precaution had been exhausted to ascertain that he was certainly dead. He related the foregoing circumstance to his attending physician during his last illness, doubtless, for the purpose of putting him upon his guard against a premature announcement of his decease.†

It would be a tedious task to follow Mr. D. in his constant attendance upon the courts, throughout the wide range of his practice; nor would the recital of his professional conflicts and achievements be very interesting to the

---

*Life and Letters of Joseph Story. Vol. 1., page 415.

†Gov. Johnson, who happened to be at Washington, and who visited Mr. D. a day or two before he died, adds, in the letter referred to in a preceding page: "That, warned by this occurrence, Mr. D. had charged his friends not to bury him hastily when his death should occur. I stated this to the physician who attended him during his sojourn in Washington, who replied that Mr. D. had made the same statement to him and others. The several physicians present, said there was no doubt of his death at this time; yet, to satisfy his absent family and friends, the large crowd assembled to attend his funeral, among whom were the President, Heads of Departments, &c., dispersed, and re-assembled on the following day, when the burial took place in the congressional cemetery. I enclosed a lock of his hair to his family; and I believe I was the only man in the city, from his district, at the time of his death."

general reader. It must suffice, for this rapid sketch, to say, that his reputation as a jurist and advocate, steadily increased as long as he lived; and that, at the time of his death, there was, perhaps, no abler lawyer in the United States. The same writer in the *American Pioneer*, already quoted (Dr. S. P. Hildreth) says:

"Mr. Doddridge, as is well known to the early inhabitants of Western Pennsylvania and Virginia, was, for many years, one of the most noted men in that region for his splendid talents at the Bar; and has, probably, never been excelled, if he has been equalled, in his discrimination in fathoming the depths of an intricate case, or in his powerful and logical reasoning in unfolding it."

Nearly the last appearance of Mr. Doddridge at the Bar in Western Virginia, in a case of importance, was in Morgantown, in April, 1829. It was upon the trial of an issue out of chancery, in the somewhat celebrated case of Ice *vs.* Ice, sent from Clarksburg to Monongalia county to be tried at the bar of the old Superior Court, before Judge Daniel Smith. The issue involved the validity of certain deeds executed by the father of the litigants to the defendants; and the facts to be ascertained were, whether, at the time of their execution the vendor was of sound mind and memory, and whether they had not been procured by undue and corrupt influences. Mr. D. was of counsel for the plaintiff. His reputation attracted an immense concourse of people, and the court house was filled with ladies and gentlemen. The character of the case afforded a fine field for the display of his peculiar and extraordinary abilities. The witnesses on both sides were numerous; and, as is usual in such controversies, their testimony was very conflicting. He made no written notes either of the testimony, or of the speeches of the opposing counsel; but not a fact disclosed, nor a point made in the case, escaped his attention or his memory. His argument was comparatively brief; but it was brilliant, complete and overwhelming. The jury returned a verdict for his client, and against the validity of the deeds.

It will not be an inappropriate conclusion to this outline of the professional career of Mr. Doddridge, to insert here an extract of a letter from him to a young man who had received permission to read law in his office, shewing his manner of instructing students, and directing their course of Study:

"WELLSBURG, 20th November, 1831.

" DEAR SIR:

"I approve, highly, the course you have marked out for yourself. To that course, however, I would make one addition. Blackstone's Commentaries is an elementary historical work, containing as well the philosophy as the history of legal science, and can be studied by one acquainted with the Latin language, as well at any other place, as in a lawyer's office. My course has been to send a Latin scholar through that book without any current assistance, directing him to keep a note-book of every thing which he does not perfectly understand. After the student is through that work, I explain the subject of his notes, and then put him through a close examination on every subject in the work.

"No student ever spent too much time on this book, and he who wishes to excel, will omit nothing in it, not even what respects church and witchcraft, or anything else, however foreign it may seem to our institutions, manners and government. At this time of your life, and in the infancy of your experience, I cannot make you sufficiently sensible how much it adds to the confidence, ease and ornament of the counsellor and advocate, to be perfectly possessed of legal history, and to be able to connect it with the general history of the mother country, and the peculiar spirit of the age in which each important change in the laws has occurred.

"Throughout this work, words used in apposition to each other, or contrasted, or by way of contradistinction, should be closely attended to. There is nothing about which that inimitable author has been more careful. For

want of attention to this particular, it is as common to hear men of our profession confounding *social* and *natural*, *municipal* with *national*, as it is to hear
them coupling a plural nominative with a verb in the singular number.

"I therefore advise that with the course of reading you propose, you
take, also, these Commentaries, appropriating to the latter the morning of
each day."

IN THE VIRGINIA LEGISLATURE.

The first important official position filled by Mr. Doddridge, so far as we have ascertained, was that of a member of the House of Delegates of Virginia, for the year 1815–16. He represented the extreme North-west point of the State—Brooke county. North Western Virginia was then, comparatively, *terra incognito*; and both its people and their political rights found very limited recognition in the exclusive and aristocratic sentiment of the Tide-water and Piedmont districts of the State. At this time, when Virginia was spoken of, it meant that part of her territory lying east of the Blue Ridge. Nevertheless, the abilities of Mr. Doddridge commanded a respect not usually extended to members from his section. He was placed on the Committee on Courts of Justice; also, on the Committee of Finances; and during the session, was added to the Committee on Taxes on Lands, &c. The journals of the House exhibit ample evidence of his industry, activity and influence during the session. It was at this session, he commenced his opposition to the arbitrary and oligarchical principles of the then existing constitution of Virginia, which he never relaxed, until the convention of 1829–30 crowned his efforts in behalf of popular rights with partial success.

He was again a member of the House of Delegates from Brooke for the year 1822–3; and was again assigned to its most important committees, viz: On Courts of Justice; On Finance; and On Schools and Colleges: and was added to the Committee on Roads and Internal Navigation. It is not often that the same member, in a body so numerous as was the House of Delegates is required to serve on so many committees at the same time.

During this session he manifested a lively interest in the promotion of education, both in the University of Virginia. and in the primary schools. The proceedings of the Legislature shew many evidences of his intelligent and effective attention to the business of the House. An eminent member of the Bar, now residing in Richmond, in a letter to the compiler of these notes, writes: *

"During this session, his prominence and influence are unmistakably conspicuous as a leader, *quasi primus inter pares;*" and adds: " You will recall, I dare say, what this means in that age of the Legislative history of Virginia. I think of a genius, inferior to none, yet known to none, because he was from the distant, unknown, and, therefore, unappreciated West."

The debates in the State Legislatures, at that early day, were rarely fully reported, and now nearly all we know of them, is contained in the brief and cursory notices of them found in the public journals of that day: and it is very seldom that one of these has been preserved. A few fragmentary synopses of some of the arguments made by Mr. Doddridge at this session of the Legislature, have been rescued from the meager relics of the past; and although they are, evidently, very imperfect, yet they bear the impress of his

* James Neeson, Esq.

vigorous mind, and have something of the ring of his incisive style.   To save the following fragment from oblivion, it
is recorded here at length.   It will shew with what comprehension and philosophy Mr. Doddridge discussed questions
of even secondary importance; and it will, at least, create
a regret that we cannot have the speech as he actually delivered it.

A Bill reducing the pay of members of the Legislature,
being under consideration, Jan. 20th, 1823, Mr. Doddridge
said :

" He would take that occasion to explain his opposition to the principles of
the bill.   He said, general objections to the bill were of a nature to render
the form of the bill, or the time of its operation, indifferent.   To what has
been said on that part of the subject, which affects the present members of the
Assembly, their officers and servants, he had only to say, they came here, and
undertook the services under the law which fixed their wages; and this is a
permanent law.   It fixed their *per diem* allowance at four dollars.   There
may be a majority who are willing to look back and reduce the allowance
from the commencement of the session; and contend for the right to impose
this on the minority.   This may be just towards some, and unjust towards
others.   There are numbers in this House who know their labors to be worth
four dollars per day, and may take it with a clear conscience.   If there are
others who know themselves to be worth less, let them, as honest men, take
less.   No law will compel them to put their hands into the Treasury and
take that which they know they have never earned.   His objections, however,
were to reduction, on grounds hitherto unnoticed in debate here.   In every
society there exists, and will ever exist, what may be called, as to wealth, at
least, three estates.   These are the wealthy sons of luxury and ease; those in
more moderate circumstances, whose continued and unremitted exertions, are
necessary for the comfortable support of themselves and families; and a third,
the poor, without the means of public or private instruction, and for that reason unqualified for legislative service.   This middle class includes the substantial yeomanry of the country, the members of a laborious profession, and
the vigilant mechanic; it is the marrow and backbone of the nation.   One
of the members from Augusta will recognize this—a truth which he will admit and, perhaps, his own identical language; and yet is himself a friend to

reduction. Either he, or some other member, is of opinion that the friends of our literary chain, erred in first providing for the first and last links. The primary schools for the assistance of the poor and wretched, and the University for the already opulent, and the first fruit of the literary fund ought to have been expended in academies and colleges for the use of the middle classes. Superior wealth has its influence upon the possessor. And this, whether it comes by descent or speedy acquisition. Its fruits are pride and arrogance, with sloth and idle habits. The sons of luxury have every advantage in the means of the most embellished education; but almost from the mother's breast, they are taught that they are not bound to look to their own exertions for future support, and from the want of this stimulus to exertion, contract, in early life, those notions of authority and habits of idleness, that disqualify them for useful and active employment here. On the other hand, the means of reasonable education for their offspring, are in the hands of most of the middle class. Their sons are taught from their youth to depend on their own exertion. These they find to be indispensable to the support of themselves and families. Their lives and habits qualify them for active services; and they have been from all time here, what they are now, and ever will be, the active, useful, and laborious class in this House. Virginia has heretofore possessed a large and controlling aristocracy of wealthy families. A powerful remnant still exists, and part of it always here. It is ever ready to act on the other classes, nor ever wittingly yields to a growing equality. In the session of 1815, this aristocracy saw a leveling principle in the scheme of universal literature then under consideration; and it could not well bear the idea, that the public hand should administer to the sons and daughters of poverty, wretchedness and misfortune, those streams of instruction which they held for their own children in their own hands, and thus a more practical equality should be introduced. To every scheme of general public instruction, the members of this ancient aristocracy, gave, in this House, a manly, able, and steady opposition; and this, the journals of that noble session will prove. In the session of 1820, an attempt like the present was made; and then, as now, it was favored by the influence of wealth. The middle class is too numerous for them, and too independent, and too incorruptible to be led. The miserable, the ignorant and dependent, would make them better tools. While they cannot but respect it, they know and feel the superior weight of the middle class; and it is not in nature that they can look upon it with much complacency. If ever they can reduce the wages so low, that the great body of the middle class cannot afford to serve, they will succeed in reducing its numbers and influence. In the session of 1820, some of them were magnanimous enough to propose such a reduction of travelling wages, as almost to abolish that part of the pay. By this means, a member who lived so near as to be able to visit his family continually, and to supervise his own concerns, saw in the offer to relinquish four or five dollars for travelling wages, an immense boon to popularity. It is not true that the present wages are too high. Gentlemen to be fit for those seats, must be men whose exertions at home, are worth something—men whose life and industry, constitute the all of their families, and who by continually serving here for their mere expenses, are doing that which, consistently with their duties at home, they cannot long support. I appeal, said he, to most of the members of the bar, and of the agricultural classes now present, and ask them if they do not know, and feel the truth of these remarks? I ask them if they feel themselves able to serve as long as their constituents wish them? and if they are not obliged to decline service, in order to protect, feed and clothe their families? If they answer for themselves as I know from experience they must, let them enquire, why will they pass this bill, and in doing so, commence a course of legislation calculated to lessen that class in whose hands the founders of our constitution placed the roots of power? and to bring into these seats an odious moneyed aristocracy? Such must, in fact, be the consequences and tendency of unreasonable reduction. They can afford it. Their labor is done, and their business is supervised by others. They are able to make of life a frolic, and can as well spend their winters and money here as at any other place of enjoyment. These considerations ought to be a warning to the middle class, to take no measures which can have the most remote tendency to lessen their own powers and influence in this body politic. But there is another argument which forcibly addresses itself to several gentlemen in the House. A certain gentleman has lately written a letter intended for the public eye. He asserts what is obviously true, that in free governments, there will always be parties; and recommends the old denomination of Whig and Tory as the most safe. However this may be, the 'ins and outs' will generally form the real parties.

"But there is now forming a party who consider themselves the exclusive friends of State Rights. This party, doubtless, contains many high-minded and honorable men—men who really fear, and others who feign to fear, that the legitimate rights of State Governments are in danger. This party sees, or thinks it sees, in the General Government and engulphing power—a power, which, acting through the executive, legislative and judicial branches, is quietly arriving at consolidation, and about to sink the State governments into those of prostrate corporations. This party found some of these fears in the decisions of the Supreme Court, in the cases of *McCulloch* vs. *Maryland*, and *Cohens* vs. *Virginia*. His opinions respecting this party was immaterial; nor would he express them further than to admit a doubt of some of the arguments in the latter case. But he would address himself to the exclusive friends of State Rights, and endeavor to convince them, that by the measure under consideration, they are accelerating the evil they would deprecate. They, by their parsimony, are bringing State employments into popular contempt. The most ignorant parts of the community can compare sums of money, and, by habit, learn to estimate public servants. like other agents, by their wages. And, therefore, the comparison of merit, or excellence, by this standard becomes both a delicate and dangerous matter. The people are reconciled, and very justly, with the salary of the President, 25,000 dollars; yet you can scarcely prevail upon yourselves to give 2,900 dollars to embellish and furnish your Governor's palace. The salaries of the Federal Judges are placed at 4,500 dollars; and you will draw tight the purse-strings, rather than pay a State Judge 2,000 dollars. And this, too, for similar services not less arduous nor longer protracted. Surely the whole society knows that judges in both governments are men who are born and educated for the same ends, have the same prospects of life, pressed by the same necessities—obliged to encounter the same necessities, and liable, at all times, to the same adverse or prosperous gales. The Federal Judge can live at a greater expense ; can support his household in a superior style; and all this passes habitually before the eyes of the multitude. When the people elect one of their neighbors to Congress, and another to the House, although until the election, they may have equal talents and equal virtues, the mind imperceptibly draws a line of discrimination between them according to the different compensation given them. The continual practice of parsimony in the State governments. compared with the liberal allowance made for the same kind of services, to the officers of the General Government, is calculated, by degrees, to increase the respect felt for the latter, in the same degree that it is calculated to degrade the former. It would be no degradation to the present General Assembly, to enquire whether the same talents and experience are now employed in it that were constantly exhibited from the Revolution until the time of the present Government of the United States, and shortly after, or even in the noble Assembly of 1815? If a difference is acknowledged, to what causes is that difference to be ascribed? Surely, to the superior allure-

ments, salaries and honors, held out and conferred by the National Government. Whatever might be our opinions drawn from speculation, our experience removes all doubt. This experience teaches us a lesson in this House
in every session. Young members appear and serve a year or two; until by
habit and practice they begin to be qualified for legislation. No sooner are
they convinced of this, than State legislation becomes to them a matter of
little importance — a dull, homely pursuit. They turn their eyes to another
city, behold the splendor and allurements of our great National Establish-
ment, and sigh for distinction in the National Government. We have heretofore seen many of them in this Hall, voting for the reduction of the wages
of all our public functionaries, including the pay of themselves and their
successors here, to an humble pittance for economy's sake, at the very moment when they are candidates for seats in the National Legislature, where
they expect, and willingly receive, a double—nay, almost a treble compensation. Think you these pecuniary distinctions fall without effect on the
public mind? No! Like the drop that ceaselessly falls, they fall upon our
feelings, until like that drop they wear into a stone. The gentlemen whom
he was now in a particular manner addressing, had always feared, or affected
to fear, the weight of National patronage. They ought to remember that
this patronage necessarily increases with the increase of territory and population. Its most alluring gifts are those of foreign diplomacy. The recognition of the new South American Governments have increased these to a
number, perhaps, equal to those in the gift of any European monarch; while
their own system of talismanic economy furnish to the State governments no
countervailing increase of influence; but is calculated to degrade the State,
and by comparison, to exalt the national authorities. Mr. Doddridge said
he had attempted to show, what we all know, the existence of a moneyed aristocracy in our State; the actual hostility of that aristocracy to the equality
which must be the fruit of every system of public instruction including the
poor; their consequent labors to aggrandize the University, and feeble efforts
to protect the primary system, and also, in their steady efforts to drive the
most numerous classes of society from honorable State employment, by a miserable parsimony. If these things are apparent, the classes who are the vic-
tims of this parsimony should tread cautiously in the path of State degradation."

Mr. Doddridge was a zealous friend and persistent advocate of education—especially, of the masses—the "the sons

of want and wretchedness," as he was apt to denominate
them. The aristocratic hostility to such education, was
still prevalent in Virginia; and we have seen, in the speech
just quoted, with what indignation he denounced this selfish
and anti-republican policy. At a subsequent day of this
session, when a bill, granting a loan to the Virginia University was under consideration, he offered an amendment to
it, providing for the more efficient operation of the system
of primary schools. He supported his amendment in a
speech of characteristic force and ability, avowing his deep
sense of the importance of popular education. He said he
" was aware of the conflict of opinion that would ensue upon
the amendment offered by him;" but he was ready to meet
it. He said that his "conduct had shewn him as unqualified a friend of the University as any man in that House.
But he was equally the friend of that system of education
which embraced the poor and the needy. And if he was to
give succor only to one of them, he should unquestionably
award it to the primary schools." He spoke of the importance of elementary education to society, in its connection
with colleges and academies, and through them, with the
University. The whole system was intimately connected.
The University and the primary schools were, but in fact,
the extreme links in the same chain. The success of the
whole, depended materially, upon the union of the several
parts. In conclusion, he "declared his determination not
to vote for a cent to the University, unless something was
done in aid of primary education."

The constitution of Virginia, as it then existed, contained
no provision disfranchising persons guilty of fighting a duel.
The progress and force of Christian civilization, had, however, so far prevailed, as to secure a statutory enactment

disqualifying those who should engage in this barbarous, and felonious practice, from holding certain offices. It seems, however, that not a few of the "hot bloods" of the State, had so disqualified themselves; and a kind of *omnibus* bill was introduced into the Legislature, relieving a considerable number of them from the penalty of the law. In support of this bill, its advocates had assimilated it to bills of amnesty, relieving those who had been engaged in civil war; and attempted to strengthen their appeal, by stating, that in some instances, the guilty act had been committed whilst the parties were students at college. Mr. Doddridge could not allow arguments so specious and fallacious to pass unnoticed. He said the

" Friends of the bill, could not avail themselves of the precedents which have been set in the acts of amnesty, which had been extended in other countries to Treason. In the commotions of civil war, men were compelled to join either one party or the other, and that too, frequently, without the means of knowing which was right, or of ascertaining which was the stronger, or which would be successful. If, in some cases, a general act of amnesty were not passed, half, or probably more than half of the nation must be sacrificed; when public justice would be as well satisfied by the execution of a few of the principal characters. He referred to the circumstances connected with the insurrection in Pennsylvania, in 1794, and the principles of policy which induced General Washington to grant, upon certain conditions, an act of amnesty to the great body of the offenders. Do the applicants, he asked, pretend to liken their cases to that in which the numbers of the offenders, and the degree of public excitement were so great as to endanger the liberties of the country? As well might a combination of murderers present themselves, and claim to be pardoned on account of their numbers. The argument, he said, could not avail. It had been stated that some of the offences had been committed at college. This, he thought, was a strong reason against relief. Youth do not reason far forward; and knowing that offences committed at college had been pardoned, would not so sensibly feel the terror of the law in that situation in which they would be most apt to violate it."

These remarks of Mr. Doddridge are valuable, not so much because they expose the sophistry of the reasons urged in extenuation of the offence which had been committed by the parties seeking relief, as for the bold and emphatic language in which the turpitude of the offence itself is denounced. Mr. Doddridge classifies the duelist with murderers: and this is, clearly, a proper classification. And since this relic of barbarism seems to be assuming renewed prevalence and proportions in some sections of the country, it may not be amiss to briefly analyse and exhibit its true character. Surely death by the duel can be nothing less than murder. The laws of the country—of every civilized country—prohibit it. The law of God condemns it. And more than this, and to leave the duelist without excuse, the civil laws make ample provision for the vindication of every man's honor and reputation. But he withdraws himself from their protection, and voluntarily exposes his own life. whilst he seeks to destroy the life of another. Ordinarily. he is a coward, too. True courage is the offspring of moral principle. It cannot exist in the absence of a sense of moral rectitude in the bosom of the actor. Its distinguishing characteristic is inflexible adherence to what is right, and unconquerable opposition to what is wrong. That dueling is wrong, every man's moral sense must testify, who has any moral perception. The attempt to justify it on moral principles, would itself, be an offence. Public sentiment is appealed to by the abettors of the duel. But the public sentiment that justifies it, or requires it, must necessarily be a false sentiment. It finds no warranty in reason, in justice, or in common sense. And he who imperils his own life, or seeks to imbrue his hands in the blood of his fellow-being, lest his courage should be impeached, precisely illustrates the difference between a false and true courage, and is guilty of moral cowardice. Whenever his courage is inspired by passion, or a spirit or motive of personal revenge, as is not unfrequently the case, it is, like the ferocity of the wild beast, simply brutal. The duelist is doubly criminal. He imperils two lives; and partakes largely of the character both of the suicide and the assassin. It is true he fights according to prescribed regulations, upon equal terms and with equal arms. But this only augments the atrocity of the offence, as forethought and deliberation aggravate the guilt of any other kind of homicide. The intention to maim or to kill, is deliberately conceived; and this constitutes the fundamental element in the crime of murder—or any other crime. The folly, too, of this species of mortal combat, is as patent as its criminality. What redress will the death of the offending party afford to the person aggrieved, for the insult, or wrong complained of? And how is a man's honor vindicated, by allowing the offending party to shoot him down?

"Am I to set my life upon a throw
"Because a bear is rude and surly? No!
"A moral, sensible, well bred man,
"Will not insult me, and no other can."

When Hamilton met Burr, he reserved his own fire, and passively received the death-shot of his antagonist. He had the courage to refuse to take the life of his enemy; but he had not the courage to face the odium which a vicious public opinion might fix upon him, if he refused to allow his enemy to destroy his life. A celebrated officer of the British army, who never had felt unmanly fear, and who had led the forlorn hope in many a desperate battle, was challenged to mortal combat by another officer. He declined. When the challenging party next met him, he spit in his face and denounced him as a coward. The recipient of the base insult deliberately wiped off the filthy spittle, and calmly said: "Could I remove the stain of your blood from my soul as readily as I do this insult from my face, it would not long remain unavenged." There was true courage. Washington, in an unguarded moment, insulted another, and was prostrated for it by a blow. Instead of calling his assailant to "the field of honor," falsely so called, he sent for him and made an apology. This, also, was genuine courage.

Nothing can be plainer than that the duelist is not only a criminal of the deepest dye, but that, in nine cases out of ten, he is deficient in moral courage; and it is to be hoped that an advanced Christian civilization will soon declare him an out-law, and banish him, like Cain, as a vagabond from the pale of society.

Shakespeare makes even a heathen utter fitting words of condemnation:

" Your words have took such pains, as if they labored
" To bring manslaughter into form, set quarreling
" Upon the head of valor; which, indeed,
" Is valor misbegot, and came into the world
" When sects and factions were but newly born:
" He's truly valiant that can wisely suffer
" The worst that man can breathe; and make his wrongs
" His outsides; wear them like his raiment, carelessly;
" And ne'er prefer his injuries to his heart,
" To bring it into danger."—*Timon of Athens.*

Mr. Doddridge suffered no appropriate occasion to pass, without manifesting his abhorence of this miserable custom. Subsequently, in the constitutional convention of 1829–30. he exerted himself to secure the insertion of a clause in the new constitution, disqualifying persons guilty of dueling , from holding office—remarking, that "he should consider it a blessing to have all doubts of a constitutional kind removed from the act, [the dueling act then existing], and to see the law and public opinion moving harmoniously together."

And again, in the House of Representatives of the United States, he strongly rebuked certain attempts to rescue "from infamy and contempt the crime of dueling—a crime which is, at once a violation of the laws of God and man; a relic of barbarous times; the refuge and resort of the base coward, more frequently than the deliberate brave."— (Speech in the Houston case.)

Mr. Doddridge was again elected to the House of Delegates and served during the winter of 1828–9. He was placed on the following important committees, viz: On Courts of Justice; On Finance; On Schools and Colleges; and On Banks.

The freeholders of Virginia, having, in pursuance of the act of the previous General Assembly, voted in favor of the call of a convention to amend the constitution of the State, it became necessary to make provision at this session, for the election of the members of the convention, and all the requisite regulations for its organization. The bill introduced for this purpose, led to a protracted and animated discussion, in which Mr. Doddridge took an active and prominent part. The principles of government, distinguishing the public opinion of the eastern and western sections of the State from each other, which afterwards became the subject of the great debate in the convention, pressed themselves into the controversy on this bill. Looking to the future, and foreshadowing the effort which he

would make in the convention, to base representation upon
the white population, and secure to the west the legislative
power to which such a basis would entitle it, Mr. Doddridge
offered a resolution to "take a census, or enumeration
of the people of the commonwealth." The astute leaders
of the dominant party, aware of the comparatively rapid
increase of white inhabitants west of the Blue Ridge, and
correctly comprehending the purpose of the resolution, defeated it by a vote of 105 for its rejection against 87 for its
adoption. The speech made by Mr. Doddridge on this occasion, was one of great ability. A pretty full report of it,
may be found in *The Richmond Enquirer*, of which there is a
file in the Congressional Library at Washington. It is probable that this is the only copy extant. It is said to have
produced a profound impression on the General Assembly,
alarming the advocates of exclusive privileges and monop-
oly of legislative power, by the unexpected manifestation
of argument and intellectual capacity, with which the west
would be prepared to meet them at the ensuing convention.

The sectional excitement between the North and the South,
which culminated in the nullification laws of South Carolina,
and the consequent famous proclamation of President Jackson, had begun, already, to seriously agitate the country;
and at this session of the Legislature of Virginia, a series of
resolutions, called "The Tariff Resolutions," was introduced
relating to the questions which distinguished the parties to
the controversy. The first of these was as follows:

"*Resolved*, That the constitution of the United States, being a Federal
compact between sovereign States, in construing which no common arbiter
is known, each State has the right to construe the compact for itself."

These resolutions were called up, on motion of Mr. Doddridge, who addressed the House at length in opposition,

especially to the one just quoted. Our researches have
failed to discover a copy of his speech. Perhaps it was
never published. The debate continued a week, principally
confined to replies to Mr. Doddridge. Nor were his opponents satisfied with these replies on the floor of the House.
Such was the force of his arguments, that it was deemed
necessary to review them in the public journals of the day.

These resolutions were adopted by a vote of 134 ayes
against 68 nays. It is hardly necessary to state that Mr.
Doddridge's vote was recorded in the negative; for he was
of the political school of Hamilton and Marshall, and of
Madison too, if we are to interpret his opinions by his letters to Mr. Trist, Mr. Everett and others, explanatory of
the purport and purpose of his celebrated report on the
Virginia Resolutions of 1798–9.

Through all the services of Mr. Doddridge in the Legislature, he kept steadily in view the primary purpose that
induced him to accept a seat in it—namely, the amendment
of the State constitution, so as to confer equal political and
personal rights on the people of every section of the State.
Nor did he confine his labors in this respect, to the Legislature; but in the intervals of his service there, he addressed
the people from the hustings on all appropriate occasions,
and, perhaps, exerted a greater influence in securing the
call of the constitutional convention of 1829–30, than any
other person in the State.

IN THE CONVENTION.

Although Virginia boasted that one of her sons was the author of The Declaration of Independence, which asserts the great principle of American liberty, that "all men are created equal;" although the Revolutionary war had been fought in vindication of the maxim, that "Taxation without Representation is Tyranny;" and notwithstanding the Bill of Rights on which she had founded her political institutions, had distinctly announced that "all men are by nature, equally free and independent;" that "all power is vested in, and consequently derived from the people;" and that "no man, or set of men, are entitled to exclusive or separate emoluments, or privileges from the community, but in consideration of public services," there still lingered even down to the period of which we are writing, in the Tidewater and Piedmont districts of the State, much of the spirit of aristocracy and oligarchy, which the colonial gentry had brought over from the mother country.

During the convention, of which we are presently to treat, one of its most distinguished members[*] spoke of the laboring classes in the western part of the State, as mere "peas-

---

[*] Benjamin Watkins Leigh, in his speech on the basis of representation.

antry"—holding the "same place in political economy as the slaves" of the east; and contemptuously inquired, "What real share, so far as mind is concerned, does any man suppose the peasantry of the west—that peasantry, which it must have when the country is completely filled up with day-laborers as ours is of slaves—can, or will take in affairs of State?"

Mr. Jefferson had animadverted on this anti-republican sentiment, in terms of commendable severity, in a letter to a friend in 1816.

Referring to a draught of a constitution he had once prepared, he said: "At the birth of our Republic, I committed that opinion to the world, in a draught of a constitution annexed to the Notes on Virginia, in which a provision was made for a representation permanently equal. The infancy of the subject at that moment, and our inexperience of government, occasioned gross departures in that draught from genuine republican canons. In truth, the abuses of monarchy had so filled all the spaces of political contemplation, that we imagined everything republican that was not monarchy. We had not yet penetrated into the mother principle, that 'governments are republican, only as they embody the will of the people and execute it.' Hence our first constitutions had really no principle in them. But experience and reflection have more and more confirmed me in the particular importance of the representation then proposed. * * * * * Reduce your Legislature to a convenient number for full, but orderly discussion. Let every man who fights or pays, exercise his just and equal right in their election."

For many years, the inequalities of representation, and the restrictions upon the right of suffrage, as regulated and prescribed by the constitution of Virginia, had been the source of bitter strife and sectional animosities, especially in those divisions of it lying west of the Blue Ridge.

Yielding, at last, to the persistent demand for reform in these respects, the Legislature of 1828, passed an act, submitting to the people, or rather, to the freeholders, of Virginia, the question: "Shall there be a convention to amend the constitution of the commonwealth?" The vote on this proposition was taken at the general election held in April of that year, resulting in a decisive majority in favor of it. And thereupon, by another act passed February 10th, 1829, provision was made for holding an election in the succeeding May, for four delegates to the convention from each of the twenty-four senatorial districts of the State. At this election Philip Doddridge, Charles S. Morgan, Alexander Campbell, and Eugenius M. Wilson, were chosen from the district composed of the counties of Ohio, Tyler, Brooke, Monongalia and Preston.

The convention met, and was organized at the capitol in the city of Richmond, on the 5th day of October, 1829. A more august and remarkable body of men, perhaps, never graced the halls of a deliberative assembly. James Monroe, ex-president of the United States, was called to the chair. Before him sat James Madison, who, also, had been president of the United States—"the father of the constitution" of the nation. There also was John Marshall, Chief Justice of the United States—"the illustrious expounder of the constitution." There, too, was Philip P. Barbour, worthy to succeed Mr. Monroe as president of the convention, when the ill health of the latter compelled him to resign. There was John Randolph of Roanoke, eager to hurl the shining shafts of his wit and invective against any one rash enough

to assail his principles, his prejudices or his passions; and
Benjamin Watkins Leigh, the chivalrous and accomplished
champion of the eastern aristocracy; and Abel P. Upshur,
prompt with his metaphysical acumen to pierce the shield
of any unwary adversary; and Charles Fenton Mercer, of
whom it was difficult to say whether he was most to be ad-
mired for the qualities of his mind, or of his heart: and
Littleton W. Tazewell, than whom, few men could bring
greater powers of intellect into the discussions, whenever he
saw proper to exert himself; and Chapman Johnson, who,
though he was vehement in manner, was no less strong in
debate, and still stronger in the moral power of his exalted
personal character; and Edwin S. Duncan, one of the ablest
judges of the general court; and Philip C. Pendleton, adding lustre to a name already historic; and John Tyler, afterwards president of the United States; and William B.
Giles, feeble from ill health, but strong in the reputation of
a long and distinguished public life; and Robert Stanard,
chosen by a district where he did not live, distinguished already for intellectual ability, soon to be crowned with the
highest judicial honors of the commonwealth; and Briscoe
G. Baldwin, rapidly rising to eminence, combining in the
fine elements of his character the richest qualities of the
heart with the highest mental endowments—likewise des-
tined to adorn the supreme bench of his State: and John
Y. Mason, bearing a venerated name, whose future career
was to reflect honor on his country, both at home and abroad;
and Alfred Harrison Powell, of manly personal presence,
of "frank and refined address," an expert parliamentarian,
and rich in intellectual resources; and William Henry Cabel,
and John W. Green, and subsequently John Coalter, orna-
ments of the bench—and worthy of the ermine they wore;

and Lewis Summers, somewhat disqualified for forensic display by the habits of the bench, but possessing a large intellect naturally judicial in its character—a capable man, and worthy of such associates; and Alexander Campbell, the eminent theologian, astute, ready, learned, able, eager to break a lance with any champion,—wanting experience only, in the new sphere in which he now appeared, to entitle him to be classed with the foremost men in the convention; and Robert B. Taylor, virtually ostracised and driven from the convention for his inflexible fidelity to the principles of human liberty and equality:

> "More true joy Marcellus exiled feels,
> "Than Cæsar with a Senate at his heels."

But the roll of distinguished names is too long to be called through. With a juster pride than that which filled the breast of the Roman matron, might Virginia have pointed to this assembly of her sons, as "jewels" worthy of the "mother of States and statesmen." It was in such a body of men that Mr. Doddridge took his seat—men illustrious, in many instances, not only for the high stations of honor and trust which they had filled, but for the distinguished manner in which they had filled them—men of world-wide reputation—eminent in the measure of their intrinsic abilities, and fortified by the experience and prestige of their exalted official positions. Mr. Doddridge came among them almost unheralded, unsupported by any of these extrinsic advantages; but he came to establish his right to rank as the intellectual peer of them all; and before the convention adjourned this claim was generally and generously recognized.

It was well understood, that the principal subjects of controversy would be the basis of representation in the legislature, and its correlative—suffrage. The ostensible plea of the members from the Tide-water and Piedmont districts was, that property, to be protected, must be represented: that the true definition of the *jus majoris* included the element of property, as well as of persons, and that in the apportionment of representation, regard should be had to population and taxation combined. This was called " *The mixed basis.*" An effort had been made in providing for the call of the convention, in the first place, to apportion its members in the several districts, according to federal numbers, viz: that three-fifths of the slaves should be represented; and the same effort was repeated in the convention, in the apportionment of representation in the legislature. This scheme soon became distinguished by the *sobriquet*— " *The black basis.*" But the real purpose of these theories of government, was the protection of slavery. The ratio of white population in the Valley and Trans-Alleghany sections of the State, where few slaves existed, over the ratio of white population in the eastern part of it, where nearly all the slaves were owned, had been rapidly increasing for many years; and from the contiguity of the former to the free States, and from the character of their industries, it was apprehended that the number of slaves never would greatly increase there; and for this reason, fears were entertained that if representation were apportioned upon white population alone, the political power would soon pass from the slave-holders into the hands of those who had no slaves, and that this power would be abused by oppressively taxing slave property, or, perhaps, in its total abolition.

Much of the success of contemplated measures in deliberative assemblies, often depends upon the mode of their organization for the transaction of business, and especially, in the appointment and constitution of their committees, and the rules of their proceedings. Mr. Doddridge duly appreciated this fact; and he manifested a lively and active interest in the organization of the House and its committees, and in the arrangement of their procedure. On the second day of the session, he introduced a series of resolutions in that behalf, which he had the satisfaction of hearing substantially reported to the convention by a special committee of twenty-four, to whom they had been referred.

Mr. Doddridge was placed upon the committee appointed to consider The Legislative Department of the Government. Of course, the duties of this committee involved the consideration of the controverted questions of suffrage and representation. The committee made a report, through Mr. Madison, on the 24th of October, consisting of thirteen resolutions, largely confined to the enunciation of elementary principles. Of these, we have the authority of Mr. Doddridge himself* that he was the author of the 1st, 2nd, 4th and 5th. The first resolution was as follows:

"*Resolved, That in the apportionment of representation in the House of Delegates, regard should be had to white population exclusively.*"

When this report was subsequently taken from the table for consideration, Judge Green moved to strike out the word "*exclusively,*" and insert instead thereof, the words—"*and taxation combined.*"

This proposition brought on a most able and interesting debate. Judge Upshur addressed the convention through a great part of two days, not only in support of this proposed amendment, in particular, but in explanation of his views of the principles and philosophy of government in general. He made an able and eloquent speech, evidently

*Letter to M. Gay, Esq., of 30th October, 1829.

the result of long thought, and careful preparation. Mr. Doddridge instantly replied to it, in an argument of signal ability, and with great effect, according to co-temporaneous notices of it. As a specimen of his style and logic, take the following extract:

"The gentleman from Northampton has labored, and I am sure he thinks successfully, to maintain that in Virginia, the majority of free white persons have not the right (and he almost denies the power) to govern the State. This *jus majoris*, he says, is not derived from the law of nature; nor from the exigencies of society; nor from the nature and necessities of government; nor yet from any conventional source, which can only be by express provision in the constitution. *Argumenti gratia*, let the gentleman be right, and for this purpose let it be conceded, that the majority could only derive this right, if at all, from some one of these repudiated sources. His conclusion, then, is, that a majority of freemen in this free land are not possessed of the right or power to govern. But government there must be, or instantly we sink into anarchy. Pray, whence, then, does the gentleman derive the power in question to the minority?"

Again:— "We have often heard that wealth gives power, or, that wealth itself is power. By this axiom I suppose is meant nothing more than the natural and moral influence which wealth gives to the possessor, by increasing his means of doing good or evil. Whenever power is directly conferred on wealth by government, the additional power thus conferred is a corrupt one. It is a *privilege* conferred contrary to the Bill of Rights, because not conferred for *merit or public services*. It is, too, an *exclusive* privilege in its *very* nature. It is an immoral distinction that is conferred, because it makes no discrimination between the possessors of estates honestly acquired, and those of ill-gotten stores."

The debate on Judge Green's amendment was continued for several weeks. An abler one is, perhaps, not to be found in parliamentary annals. The argument of Mr. Doddridge, although comparatively brief, was not surpassed in vigor, logic, or intellectual force by any other. Before a decision was reached upon the question, it was laid aside; and the convention passed to the consideration of the right of suffrage. An animated discussion ensued upon this topic, in which most of the leading members of the body participated—Mr. Doddridge among them. The committee on the Legislative Department of the Government had reported a resolution providing for a freehold, or a recorded leasehold for a term of five years, as a necessary qualification in each voter. The general sentiment of the eastern members was in favor of some such qualification. The general sentiment of the western members was, practically, in favor of what was called universal suffrage. Several amendments had been offered to the plan reported by the committee, and had been rejected by the convention, when Mr. Doddridge proposed the following:

"And shall be extended to every free white male citizen, aged twenty-one years, or upwards, who shall have resided at least one whole year in the county, city, borough, or district, in which he shall offer to vote, immediately preceding the time of voting; and who, during that period, shall actually have paid a revenue tax legally assessed—and to every free white male citizen, aged twenty-one years or upwards, who shall actually have resided at least one whole year in the county, city, borough, or district where he offers to vote; and who, for the period of six months, at least, shall have been an housekeeper therein."

It is evident from the remarks made by Mr. Doddridge when he offered this amendment, that it did not embody, exactly, his personal judgment of what should be the proper extent of suffrage; but restricted it more than he would have required, if the matter had been left to his own free determination.

His speech upon this amendment was distinguished by his usual ability. An extract or two will indicate its character.

Mr. Leigh had complained that the epithets—aristo-
- crats, and oligarchs—had been opprobiously applied to
4

those who opposed the extension of suffrage. Mr. Doddridge said : —

"The gentleman from Chesterfield says he has so far forgotten his Greek as not to remember these terms in that language, and he only knows their meaning in good old English, and not in the modern dialect of that tongue. I will in that dialect explain my meaning of both terms. They are, in fact, synonymous. Each of these terms is descriptive of a government whose powers are vested in a minority. A government thus described is contradistinguished from a monarchy, or a government in the hands of one man, and from a pure democracy in the hands of every man. By government in the hands of a few, we do not mean a small, select few. Few and many, as the gentleman from Chesterfield says, are relative terms. In their just sense, they are equivalent with the terms majority and minority. In this sense I use them. A government, to be an aristocracy, or oligarchy, is not, necessarily, one in which power is acquired by descent or patent. This is the sense in which I use the terms; and if I am correct, to constitute a statesman an aristocrat, or oligarch, it is only necessary that he should be one of those holding and exercising the power of the few over the many—of the minority over the majority."

Replying to the clamor of those who alleged that the efforts of the friends of extended suffrage were revolutionary in their character and tendencies, leading to the subversion of the peace and order of society, he said : —

"What we contemplate is not revolution. The government is an elective republic, and we mean to leave it so. Yet we are warned of the dangers and horrors of revolution. Revolutions, it is said, never stop at the objects first had in view, but the ball once set in motion, goes downward on the road to anarchy or despotism, and never stops. One false step can never be recalled; the descent to ruin is easy, but to return difficult, if not impossible: *hoc opus, hic labor est.* Could we forget where we are, and listen to the speeches of gentlemen in opposition, we should forget the business we are engaged in; we should imagine we were listening to Burke on the French Revolution. All the horrors of that volcano are set before us, as if, in our madness, we were ready to plunge into it. We are likened to the priests of France in the last age; we are called fanatics, dreamers, and even drivelers, by gentlemen of this city; the history of the ancient republics is invoked to alarm us; at one time it is said that each of these perished, when suffrage was made general, and governments established on the rights of numbers. With much more truth, we are again told that these republics, with all their temporary governments, have fallen, without leaving in their history anything for our instruction. The truth is, that neither in antiquity, nor in the ages succeeding the fall of Rome, were there any governments formed on our model; not one. Before ours, there never existed one government in the world, in which the whole power was vested in the people and exercised by them through their representatives; in which powers were divided between separate and distinct bodies of magistracy, and in which no nobility or privileged order existed. It is in vain, therefore, that we are incessantly lectured like schoolboys about the republics of Greece, Sparta, Lacedamon, Rome and Carthage. In our sense of the term, in the Virginia sense of it, neither of these was a Republic. They have perished, indeed, as all others of the same age have done, some in war and conquests, some by one cause and some by another. Perhaps among the inscrutable decrees of Providence, there is one by which all governments, like the men composing them, are to have a beginning, a maturity, and an end."

Referring to the tenacity with which men vested with power always cling to it, and the opposition which they invariably make to progress and reform, he remarked :—

"Mr. Chairman, what do we hear on this occasion, more than the alarming predictions, melancholy forebodings and evil auguries usual on every question of reform? When were men in power ever ready to reform? When did they yield power except to force or fear? We have lived to see Catholic Emancipation in Ireland, after many attempts to accomplish that measure. On each of these occasions the ministers answered according to custom; sometimes that the country was at war with France, or the whole continent; sometimes the Christian religion was in danger; and at others, that reform would jeopardize both church and State. Their predictions were never more gloomy and fearful than on the eve of Catholic Emancipation. They were of precisely the same nature, and of the same justice, with those of our opponents here. The Catholics are emancipated, and England has gained strength by that act of justice. By a similar act of political emancipation, Virginia will increase her strength and happiness, notwithstanding the forebodings of men about to part with power."

When the debate was resumed on the basis of representation, sectional feelings had begun to develop themselves
with much vehemence in the convention; and the champions of the eastern aristocracy, repulsed on the field of
argument, began to sound the tocsin of alarm, which they
so well knew how to do, and to utter angry menaces, in order to terrify the friends of popular rights into submission.
Mr. Doddridge had satisfied them that they could hope for
no advantage in fair discussion of principles; and now he
was to shew them that in moral and political courage he
was also their equal.   He met their assaults with his usual
courtesy, indeed, but with a promptness and firmness which
left no room for misapprehension.   In reply to Mr. Leigh
and Mr. Randolph, he said : —

"The gentleman from Chesterfield, in his first argument on the basis, declared that a government in this State, founded on the right of numbers
of white population, would be such a cruel, intolerable and insupportable
tyranny as no man ever did, could or would submit to. About seventy hours
since, and again to-day, that gentleman has repeated this declaration. Such,
then, is the deliberate judgment of that gentleman.   The gentleman from
Charlotte (Mr. Randolph) with equal candor declared yesterday, that any
constitution which would establish in the House of Delegates the basis of
free white numbers would be a *Jacobinical* government to which he never
could submit. Those gentlemen occupy, and deservedly, a large space in
this House, and in public opinion.   On this ground, the latter gentleman,
planted his staff and nailed his flag. As I view things, gentlemen have a
right to maintain as they do, that our doctrines tend to anarchy, despotism
or Jacobinism, and to support their opinions by fair argument: in doing so
they give no cause of personal offence. On the other hand I have a right to
maintain, that their doctrines go to build up an oligarchy of wealth. Here,
then, we stand on equal ground. In the same spirit of frankness, that an-
imates the gentleman from Charlotte, I now say, and for the last time,
that yielding us the free white basis in the House of Delegates, with
a new apportionment of representation after the next census, and periodical enumerations and apportionments, I will yield the Federal

numbers in the Senate. Further than this I will never go, and here I nail my flag."

So completely had the arguments of Mr. Doddridge, and those who concurred with him, met the theories of representation maintained by the eastern aristocracy, that they, at last practically, abandoned all their avowed principles in that behalf, and by a kind of *coup de main*, constituted both branches of the legislature by an arbitrary apportionment in the four geographical divisions of the State, corresponding neither with white population, federal numbers, or population and taxation combined; ordaining that the House of Delegates should consist of thirty-one delegates to be chosen for and by the twenty-six counties lying west of the Alleghany Mountains; twenty-five for and by the fourteen counties lying between the Alleghany and Blue Ridge of Mountains; forty-two for and by the twenty-nine counties lying east of the Blue Ridge Mountain above tide-water; and thirty-six for and by the counties, cities, towns and boroughs lying upon tide-water; and that the Senate should consist of nineteen members east of the Blue Ridge, and thirteen west thereof. It was further ordained that in the year 1841, and every ten years thereafter, the legislature should reapportion the representation in these counties, cities, towns and boroughs, but that such reapportionment should not increase the number of delegates and senators in any of the respective geographical divisions aforesaid; excepting, that after the year 1841, the General Assembly should have authority, *two-thirds of both Houses concurring*, to make periodical reapportionments of delegates and senators throughout the commonwealth, so that the number of the former should never exceed 150, nor of the latter 36. For this restriction, requiring the concurrent assent of two-

thirds of each House, Mr. Madison was principally respon-
sible. The purpose from the beginning, of the dominant
party in the convention, was, to retain the political power
east of the Blue Ridge; and this arrangement accomplished
it as effectually as organic law could do it.

Mr. Doddridge exerted himself to secure a clause in the
constitution providing for its future amendment, through
the assembling of another convention, or in some other
proper and practicable mode. But even this poor concession was refused. But all the barriers thus interposed to
arrest the progress of popular liberty have fallen; equality
of rights has triumphed at last; and now the public sentiment and the fundamental laws, not only of Eastern Virginia, but of all the States, are in advance even of the principles maintained by Mr. Doddridge and his coadjutors,
then so bitterly assailed as Jacobinical and revolutionary.

It would involve too many details and extend this sketch
beyond the limits prescribed to it, to follow Mr. Doddridge
through all his vigilant and active participation in the proceedings of the convention. Suffice it to say, that there was
no question of importance before it, which did not receive
his careful attention, and to the consideration of which, he
did not bring an intelligence and comprehension which
commanded the respect and admiration of the entire House.

A cursory reference to his opinions and speeches upon
topics and propositions before the convention, is all that
may be permitted.

Mr. Doddridge placed great stress upon an independent
Judiciary; and regarded the tenure *quamdiu se bene gesserit*
as indispensable. "I pray," said he, "that we, and our posterity to remotest time, may never be weak enough to part
with this surest, greatest sheet-anchor of every free state."

The objection to this life tenure, has always been, the difficulty of uniting with it a proper and efficient sense of responsibility—to leave the judge perfectly free to do right
according to the unbiased dictates of an upright and honest
judgment, and, at the same time, to place him under such a
sense of accountability as will deter him from doing wrong,
if he were so inclined. Influenced by this consideration,
principally, the modern practice and policy of the several
States, have been to limit the judicial office to a fixed term
of years. Whether any justly compensating advantage has
been secured, is still a problem which experience has not
satisfactorily solved beyond a reasonable doubt; and it must
be acknowledged that there is, to some extent, a reaction in
the public opinion against the experiment.

Upon the oft-mooted question whether ministers of the
gospel should be eligible to seats in the legislature, he said:
"The resolution is, that a man's religious opinions shall not
affect his civil capacities; but the proviso declares that those
opinions uttered in the pulpit shall affect his civil capacities
even to disfranchisement. At the *polls*, he should probably
act with the gentleman; but why tie up the hands of the
people?"

He was in favor of electing the Governor by the people;
taking the ground of Mr. Jefferson, that an executive appointed by the legislature made him, in fact, an emanation
of the legislative power; and was, therefore, a violation of
the fundamental principle, that the legislative, executive
and judiciary departments of the goverment should be kept
distinct, separate, and independent of each other.

Whilst not going so far, at that time, as to propose a total
abolition of the county courts, because he did not know
what were the wishes of his constituents in that behalf, he

yet insisted that they ought not to be so constituted as to be independent of the legislative will, and above that will; but that the General Assembly ought to have power to abolish them if the people and the interests of jurisprudence should require it to be done. The wisdom of this opinion was afterwards vindicated in the fact, that one of the principal causes leading to the call of the constitutional convention of 1850-51, was the public dissatisfaction with the county courts. In this, it is not improbable, that history will repeat itself in West Virginia.

The convention had now nearly completed its labors, and had agreed upon the fundamental principles which they proposed to incorporate in the new form of government; but these were contained in detached, distinct, and unconnected propositions and resolutions, adopted at different times during the session. It now became necessary, not only to classify and arrange them in their proper order, but also to give expression to them with the precision of language, perspicuity of style, and freedom from redundant verbiage, essential to the perfection of organic law. This was a delicate and difficult task. A select committee was appointed to perform it. It was a most flattering mark of the confidence of that illustrious body of men, and of their high appreciation of his qualification for so important a duty, that Mr. Doddridge was placed at the head of that committee, the other members of which, were Messrs. Madison, Marshall, Leigh, Johnson, Tazewell and Cooke; and it was more especially so, as it was known that the new constitution was to be of such a character, as when it should be completed, Mr. Doddridge could not vote for it.

It has already been stated, that it was Mr. Madison, who, from the Committee on the Legislative Department of the

Government, reported to the convention the resolution that representation in the House of Delegates should be based upon white population exclusively. The members from the western part of the State had entertained strong hopes that this proposition would prevail; but in an evil hour, Mr. Cooke, one of the original champions of the principle enunciated in the resolution, abandoned its support, on the grounds that it was impracticable to sustain it in the convention, and allied himself to the friends of the "mixed basis." Mr. Madison, if he did not exactly follow this example, relaxed his adherence to the proposition, and signified a willingness to compromise with its opponents. This was the occasion of bitter chagrin to Mr. Doddridge, who, it seems, animadverted with considerable feeling and severity upon the unexpected defection. Several years afterwards, Mr. Madison wrote to Mr. Doddridge in reference to the motives which influenced him to pursue the course he did. It is, perhaps, but an act of justice in this connection, to allow Mr. Madison to make his own explanation:

"If I were in an ill-humor with you," Mr. Madison writes, "which I am not, and never was, I might here advert to a misconstruction, which, in your controversy with Mr. Cooke, you put on the amendment I proposed in our late convention authorizing the legislature, two-thirds of each house concurring, to re-apportion the representation as inequalities might, from time to time, require. My motive, I am conscious, was pure, and the object I still think proper. The right of suffrage, and the rule of apportionment of representation are fundamentals in a free government, and ought not to be submitted to legislative discretion. The former had been fixed by the constitution, but every attempt to provide a constitutional rule for the latter had failed, and of course no remedies could be applied for the greatest inequalities without a convention, at which the general feeling seemed to revolt. In this alternative, it appeared the lesser evil to give the power of redress to the legislature, controlling its discretion by requiring a concurrence of two-thirds instead of a mere majority."

Of the whole number of illustrious men who composed
the convention, only three remain alive at this time—Mark
Alexander, of Mecklenburg, Samuel McDowell Moore, of
Rockbridge,* and Hugh Blair Grigsby, of Edgehill, near
Charlotte Court-house. In 1853, Mr. Grigsby delivered a
most eloquent discourse before the Virginia Historical Society at Richmond, entitled "The Virginia Convention of
1829–30," in which he has furnished a lively portraiture of
its distinguished members. Amongst others, Mr. Doddridge
has been honored with an appreciative tribute of his grace-
ful pen. It will afford an appropriate conclusion to this
sketch of Mr. Doddridge's participation in the proceedings
of that memorable assembly :

"With all who are conversant with the legislative history of the State,
the name of Philip Doddridge has long been familiar. Perhaps, to him more
than to any other man living, disconnected from the public press, the convention then sitting owed its existence. As early as 1816, with Smythe and
Mercer, he had fought the battle in the House of Delegates with success, but
his favorite measure was defeated in the Senate. Then, and not till then, did
he approve the passage of the bill re-arranging the senatorial districts on the
basis of white population. Although he never entirely forgave the East because the districts were re-arranged on the census of 1810, and for the loss of
a fraction of population which he thought was due to the West, he was can-
did and generous in his appreciation of the talents displayed by his opponents on that occasion; and often, in private, and more than once in debate, spoke of the arguments of Tazewell in reply to General Smythe on the
convention-bill of that session as by far the ablest he had ever heard in a deliberative assembly. A member of the House of Delegates, at intervals,
through a long tract of time, he was in that body during the session of
1828–9, when the bill calling the existing convention became a law, and sustained it with a masterly speech. It may not be unjust to the living or the
dead, to affirm that of all the distinguished representatives from beyond the
Ridge he held the first place in the estimation of the West. There his early
history was known; there his fine talents brought forth their first fruits; and

* Mr. Moore has died since the above was written.

there was the theatre in which his greatest forensic efforts were made. There was something, too, in the fortunes of a friendless youth, who, with no aid but his own untiring spirit, winning his way to the highest distinction, yet retaining to the last the simple manners of early years, which appeals to the best feelings of the human heart everywhere. The people of the West knew and loved the man, but they had known and loved the boy. The interview of the young Doddridge, chubby, sunburnt, ungainly, and in his boatman's garb, with the haughty governor of the Spanish Territory on the Mississippi—neither understanding the native language of the other, but conversing in bastard Latin which the youth had picked up while his fellows were pinking squirrels out of the tree-tops of the yet unbroken forests of the West, would form a suggestive picture, which I hope the brush of some Western son of genius will commit to canvass for the admiration of future times. Well and worthily did he requite the affection of the West. Not only in his great speech on the basis question, when the hope of triumph was bright before him, but afterwards, when his plans were thwarted, did he strive to secure the great object of his mission. As a speaker he had many great qualities—readiness, fluency, and an unlimited command of all the logic, and, what was of great importance in that body, of all the statistics of his case. Irascible even, and prompt to take offence where offence was intended, he was distinguished for great courtesy in debate;—a trait so distinctly marked as to call forth the pointed acknowedgement of Randolph. Whether he prepared himself for the occasion, I cannot say—for the whole subject had been the study of years—but in the great debate on the basis, and in the innumerable ones which would suddenly spring up, he was a gushing fountain of facts and figures. He had none of the ordinary graces of a speaker about him. His voice seemed to come from his throat, and had no freedom of play. He was low and broad in stature; his features were heavy, though to a close observer they might bespeak a great mind in repose; and in his dress he was a very sloven. Indeed, his form and dress, even his position in the Convention, as well as the powers of his great mind, are foreshadowed by Horace in his third satire as faithfully as if the Tiber and the Yohogany were sister streams:

> "*Iracundior est paulo, minus aptus acutis*
> *Naribus horum hominum; rideri possit eo, quod*
> *Rusticius tonso toga defluit, et male laxus*
> *In pede calceus hæret: at est bonus, ut melior vir*
> *Non alius quisqam, at tibi amicus, at ingenium ingens*
> *Inculto latet hoc sub corpore.*"

This estimate of Mr. Doddridge must be the more highly appreciated, since it is made, not only by a competent eye-witness of his participation in the proceedings of the convention, but, also, by one who was in direct antagonism of opinion from him upon the great questions which agitated the body—a witness, however, too generous and magnanimous to permit a difference of opinion to withhold the admiration justly due to exalted abilities. Nor has the lapse of time, and the consequent sobriety of age and reflection, abated the measure of Mr. Grigsby's admiration; for in a recent letter, addressed to Hon. Charles James Faulkner, he writes of Mr. Doddridge:

"I knew him with some degree of intimacy, such as might exist between a man of fifty and a youth of two and twenty; and I was specially impressed by the goodness of his heart, by his generous feelings, by his liberal estimation of the genius and abilities of his most formidable rivals, as I also was in his public exhibitions of his own wonderful powers. I was with him both in the House of Delegates and in the Convention of 1829–30, heard all that he uttered in both bodies, and particularly in the legislative committee of the Convention, and in each and all of his efforts I was struck with his eminent skill in debate, with the wealth of his resources, and with his great powers of argumentation. In society he was always gentle and courteous, following rather than leading the stream of talk, and delighted us all by the rapid course of his speech, and by the wisdom of his discourse. Though a federalist and an extreme upholder of the doctrines of the west when the passions were running high, he not only did not undervalue the fine qualities of his political opponents in State and federal politics, but pronounced on a distinguished opponent one of the finest compliments ever paid by one man of genius to another. I deeply deplored his death, and hold his memory in the highest reverence."

IN CONGRESS---DEATH, &C.

In 1823, Mr. Doddridge was a candidate for a seat in the House of Representatives of the United States, from what was called the Wheeling District of Virginia. At that time, the election was held, and continued, on the first day of the county courts of the respective counties composing the district, during the entire month of April. There were, that year, five competitors for the position; all of whom appeared on the hustings at Wheeling on the first Monday of April, and addressed the people, according to the custom prevailing in Virginia. It soon became apparent, however, that the contest was, in fact, between Mr. Doddridge, and Joseph Johnson, esq., of Harrison county, who still survives, who had served with Mr. Doddridge in the Legislature of Virginia, and who was then just fairly entering upon his long career of public life; and on the second Monday, all the candidates retired from the canvas, excepting Mr. Doddridge and Mr. Johnson. Mr. Johnson was one of the most popular and effective speakers who ever appeared on the hustings in Western Virginia. He also had the advantage of belonging to the dominant party; and when the voting was

concluded on the last Monday of the month, it appeared
that Mr. Doddridge was defeated, notwithstanding his acknowledged peerless abilities. In 1825 Mr. Doddridge and
Mr. Johnson were again opposing candidates for the same
position, and with the same result. In 1829, they were a
third time competitors, when Mr. Doddridge, after an animated canvas, was successful.

His duties as a member of the Virginia Convention de-
tained him in that body until its adjournment on the 15th
of January, 1830; so that he did not take his seat in the
Congress until after that time. He found himself still surrounded by several of the distinguished men of Virginia,
some of whom had served with him in the convention.
Among them, were Philip P. Barbour, William F. Gordon
and Charles Fenton Mercer; and with them John S. Barbour,
William S. Archer, and Andrew Stevenson. His reputation, acquired in the convention, had preceded him; and
he at once occupied an intellectual rank equal to that of any
of his eminent colleagues, and hardly second to any member
of the House. Especially was this so, upon all questions
involving the discussion of legal and constitutional principles. Soon his assiduous, intelligent, and effective attention to the business referred to the committees to which he
had been assigned, attracted the notice, and commanded
the confidence, of his associates. He did not often address
the House; but when he did so, he uniformly confined his
remarks to the distinct question before it, speaking with
brevity and perspicuity as well as pertinency. As a consequence, he was listened to with a respectful attention, not
often accorded to each other, by the members of that tu-
multuous assembly, and commanded the confidence and influence to which his talents entitled him. His personal

bearing, too, toward his fellow members, as it always had been toward opposing counsel at the bar, was in the best style of manly courtesy. And yet, when the occasion justified it, he could retort with great severity—all the more severe and pungent, because his retort was free from vulgarity and violence. A characteristic instance may be found in a reply he made to an ungenerous impeachment of his motives by a member from North Carolina, in debating a proposition to reduce the duty on salt. This reply will also shew his reverence for the Bible, and his abhorrence of the flippancy and levity with which public speakers sometimes bandy phrases and quotations from the sacred volume:

"I feel," said Mr. Doddridge, "compelled to take a respectful notice of the remarks of the gentleman from North Carolina (Mr. Barringer) in relation to my vote yesterday evening, and my motion to-day, which has given rise to the present discussion. The gentleman has made allusion to the treason and kiss of Judas. I am at a loss to know whether he meant to be witty or satirical. If wit was his object, he failed; for I could not see that a single smile was elicited in the hall. Should I presume, as that gentleman did, to offer an advice not asked for, I would say, that whenever he attempts to extract his sallies of wit from a record the most awful and instructive that the mind of man can contemplate, he will exhibit himself in bad taste before a Christian audience. But if satire was intended, and the gentleman meant both to assail me, and at the same time to give us a sample of his magnanimity, he was signally successful. Having cast his arrow across the hall at me, he most magnanimously demanded the previous question; which would shut my mouth from this explanation, and from a reply."

On his return home after the adjournment of the first session of the 21st Congress, he was received by his constituents with great respect and enthusiasm. His manly and brilliant vindication of popular rights in the convention, had endeared him to the hearts of the people throughout the entire north-western section of the State. A public

dinner was tendered to, and accepted by, him, at the Ma-
sonic Hall in Wheeling, on Saturday, the 3rd of July, at
which Noah Zane, esq., presided, supported by other prominent citizens as vice-presidents. Two hundred and thirteen guests sat down to the table. Wheresoever he appeared,
he was the cynosure of all eyes. Sometimes men become
suddenly popular, when no substantial grounds can be assigned for it—a kind of passionate, unreasoning excitement,
subsiding with equal rapidity, like the mountain torrent
after a storm. But the admiration of Mr. Doddridge was
an intellectual one, having its source in the judgment of
the people, resting upon the basis of unquestioned and un-
questionable abilities, and supported by important services
actually rendered.

Although the proceedings of Congress do not show that
Mr. Doddridge often participated in the discussions on the
floor of the House, his name is prominent in its journals, in
connection with the actual business of the country before
it. When, however, occasion required, he made his voice
potential. He always entertained the highest regard for
the Judiciary Department of the government; and was
ever on the alert to vindicate and protect it from encroach-
ment by the co-ordinate branches. He considered that the
Supreme Court of the United States was, after all, the
sheet-anchor of the constitution, and of the federal union.
And when an effort was made in 1831, in the interest of
those sectional antipathies which, afterwards, culminated in
flagrant rebellion, to repeal the 25th section of the judiciary
act of 1789, he startled the House by the declaration that
the proposition to do so was incipient treason. During the
debate in relation to it, he re-iterated the avowal, remarking "that much had been said, and many allusions had

been made to an expression of his on a former occasion, that he considered the proposition to repeal the 25th section of the judiciary act, as equivalent to a motion to dissolve the Union. Such," said Mr. Doddridge, "is my opinion. It is my opinion, and I hope no angry feelings will be produced by my avowing it."

It may not be uninteresting in this connection, to advert to the controverted question—who was the author of the judiciary act of 1789? It had been generally attributed to the pen of Mr. Madison. Mr. Doddridge, in a subsequent discussion upon another subject, had said: "We, in Virginia, have understood Mr. Madison to be the penman. If this is an historical error, I would like to be informed; if it is not, the foreseeing of the necessity of making such a provision, at that time, is but another proof of the great sagacity of the late president, Mr. Madison." This remark having attracted the attention of Mr. Madison, he wrote to Mr. Doddridge, under date of January 6th, 1832, as follows:

"The bill originated in the Senate, of which I was not a member, and was understood, truly I believe, to have proceeded from Mr. Ellsworth, availing himself, as may be presumed, of consultations with some of his most enlightened colleagues." He adds: "Those who object to the control given to the Supreme Court of the United States over the State Courts, ought to furnish some equivalent mode of preventing a State government from annulling the laws of the United States, through its judiciary department, the annulment having the same anarchical effect, as if brought about through either of its other departments." *

Few members, if any, in the 21st Congress, when it expired, left the halls of the Capitol with a higher reputation for all the qualities of an able representative, than Mr. Doddridge; and he was re-elected without opposition. Some of his eminent colleagues of the previous Congress were not

---

* Madison's writings, vol. 4, page 222.

returned; but several gentlemen of equal eminence were— among them, John Y. Mason, and John M. Patton. Mr. Doddridge not only maintained his former standing, but rose still higher in the estimation of the House, and of the country. Alas! before another session had convened, death, who "ever loves a shining mark," had claimed him for his own.

Already, in the history of the country, the question of abolishing slavery began to agitate, and seriously disturb the councils of the nation. It is curious to observe from the stand-point of 1875, how this question was regarded by Congress in 1831. On the 12th day of December of that year, Ex-President John Quincy Adams, then a member of the House, presented numerous petitions from citizens of Pennsylvania, mostly members of the society of Friends, praying for the abolition of slavery, and the slave trade in the District of Columbia. Mr. Adams, in presenting these petitions, said, that they

"Asked for two things: the first was the abolition of slavery; the second, the abolition of the slave trade in the District of Columbia. There was a traffic in slaves in the District of Columbia, which he did not know, but that it might be a proper subject of legislation for Congress. As to the other prayer of the petitions, the abolition of slavery in the District of Columbia, it occurred to him that the petition might have been committed to his charge under an expectation that it would receive his countenance and support. He deemed it his duty, therefore, to declare that it would not. Whatever might be his opinion of slavery in the abstract, or of slavery in the District of Columbia, it was a subject which he hoped might not be discussed in that House; if it should be, he might, perhaps, assign the reasons why he could give it no countenance or support. At present, he would only say to the House, and to the worthy citizens who had committed their petitions to his charge, that the most salutary medicines, unduly administered, were the most deadly of poisons."

Such were the sentiments of a Massachusetts Representative in 1831.

These petitions were referred to the Committee on the District of Columbia, of which Mr. Doddridge was a member. On the 19th of December he made a report from that committee, adverse to so much of the prayer of the petitioners as referred to the abolition of slavery—assigning as a reason therefor, the consideration that the District of Columbia was composed of territory originally ceded to the United States by the States of Virginia and Maryland, in which slavery still existed, and which entirely surrounded the District; and, therefore, it would, perhaps, be a violation of good faith towards those States, for Congress to abolish slavery in the District "until the wisdom of the State governments had devised some practicable means of eradicating or diminishing the evils of slavery of which the memorialists complained;" and further reporting that, "If under any circumstances such an interference of Congress would be justified, that the present is an inauspicious moment for its consideration." He, therefore, asked that the committee be discharged from the further consideration of so much of the petitions as prayed for the abolition of slavery in the District of Columbia. The report is silent as to the slave trade in the District.

At this time, when the Ohio river, and all of our navigable streams, are spanned from all the principal cities on their banks with bridges daily burdened with the transit of our internal commerce, it would hardly occur to the present generation, that the constitutional authority permitting their erection had ever been disputed. Yet such is the fact. Upon this point, however, the well-instructed mind of Mr. Doddridge had no difficulty. For we find, that on the 23d

of December, 1831, he offered a resolution directing "the
Committee on Internal Improvements to inquire into the
expediency of providing for the erection of a bridge over
the Ohio river at the town of Wheeling." Although this
was only a resolution of inquiry, Mr. Speight, of North Carolina, opposed its adoption, on the ground that Congress
had no constitutional authority to authorize such a structure. Mr. Doddridge declined to discuss the question on a
preliminary inquiry; but declared his readiness to sustain
the right of Congress, not only to authorize, but, if need be,
to build the bridge, whenever the proposition should prop-
erly come before the House for consideration.

The centennial anniversary of Washington's birthday was
now near at hand. A joint committee of the two Houses
had been appointed to report on the subject. They recom-
mended that there should be an adjournment of the two
Houses, from the 21st to the 23rd of the current month,
(February, 1832); that the day should be celebrated by an
oration suitable to the occasion; that John Marshall, Chief
Justice of the United States, be requested to assist in the
ceremonies of the day by delivering the oration; and that
Congress adopt the necessary measures to carry into effect
the resolution which was proposed by Congress on the 24th
day of December, 1799, for the removal of the body of
George Washington, and its interment in the capitol at the
City of Washington. It is a matter of continued regret, that
the Chief Justice was unable to comply with the request
made to him. In reply to a letter addressed to him on the
subject, he said, that:

"In addition to the pressure of official duties which occupy me entirely, and
render it impossible for me to devote so much time to the subject as its intrin-

sic importance and great interest in the estimation of the world, require, I am physically unable to perform the task I should assume. My voice has become so weak as to be almost inaudible, even in a room not unusually large. In the open air, it could not be heard by those nearest me. I would, therefore, decline the honor proposed."

Mr. Doddridge manifested a lively interest in the matter, and earnestly advocated the adoption of the report of the committee. An objection was raised, "placed upon the ground of a particular interpretation of the will of the deceased," and, also, upon a refusal understood to have been made by Judge Washington, in 1816. Mr. Doddridge, with his usual judicial discrimination, readily refuted the interpretation of the will relied on:

"He could not concur in such a view of it. He thought that entertained by Mrs. Washington was more correct. The article referred to, merely prescribed a duty to his executors. The testator could not possibly have foreseen the resolution of 1799, nor the refusal of his relative in 1816, nor the effort now making in Congress, and, therefore, could not put his own will in hostility to that of his common country. It would have been indecorous to make such a request during his lifetime. It could only take place after his death." And "he asked if it could be believed, that in answer to so humble a request Washington would have countervailed the wishes of his country."

Strange to say, the debate upon this report elicited strong sectional feeling before it was concluded. Even then, the dissolution of the Union was prognosticated. Mr. Thompson, of Georgia, said in his place: "I presume there is scarcely an individual in this hall, who does not feel compelled to look to the possibility of a severance of this Union. Indeed, some profess to think such an event is probable. God forbid," said Mr. Thompson. "May this Union be continued through all time." "But," he continued, "remove the remains of our venerated Washington from the remains of his consort and his ancestors, from Mount Ver-

non and his native State, and deposit them in this capitol,
and then let a severance of this Union occur, and behold the
remains of Washington on a shore foreign to his native
soil!" It is suggested here, that those "remains" could
hardly have slept in peace on any shore, not embraced
within the Union which he had devoted his life to create
and establish.

Mr. Doddridge replied to these unpatriotic vaticinations
with a brevity and indifference bordering on contempt.
"As to the gloomy anticipations," he said, "that this spot
was to become the frontier of two hostile nations, those
who thought more seriously of such a danger than he did,
were at liberty to speculate for themselves. He should
act for the present."

But the remains of Washington still repose beneath the
shades of his beloved Mount Vernon; and there let them
repose undisturbed forever—consecrated by the homage of
mankind—belonging not alone to Virginia, nor yet to the
whole nation, but to all the friends of virtue and human
rights throughout the world, down to "the latest syllable
of recorded time"—surrounded by a halo of glory, which
even the nation's capitol for a monument could, in nowise,
tend to enhance. The capitol, with its iron dome and massive marble columns may decay, and crumble into dust.
Some far, far future antiquarian Layard, may be found ex-
cavating among the rubbish of ages, to ascertain its site.
But the fame of Washington, imperishable as truth, will
still endure, needing nothing extrinsic to perpetuate it.

It was during this Congress, when the celebrated Samuel
Houston, afterwards the hero of San Jacinto, and president
of Texas, on the streets of Washington, assaulted Mr. Stans-
berry, a member of the House from Ohio, after its adjourn-

ment, and at a distance from the capitol, for words spoken in debate. The assault was a violent one, inflicting serious bodily injury. Mr. Houston was arrested and brought before the House for a breach of its privileges. The annals of Congress do not furnish, perhaps, an abler debate than that which ensued upon the trial of this case. The question involved being, principally, of a legal character, fell within the range of Mr. Doddridge's professional studies; and the speech he made on the occasion, may be justly ranked among the ablest forensic efforts of which there is any record. And yet the author of this sketch used to hear members of the bar, with whom Mr. Doddridge practised, say, that it was only an average example of his arguments in important cases.

The speech is hardly susceptible of analysis; for it is, itself a simple and severe analysis: and is so perfect in its arrangement, and compact in its structure, as to render the facts stated and principles applied inseparable from the conclusions deduced. It would be difficult to make a synopsis, shorter than the argument; and yet the argument is full, clear and conclusive. The main argument, however, is prefaced with a review of the history of parliamentary privileges, generally, and of the particular privilege in question, more especially, in which, occupying only two or three pages, the reader will find, perspicuously stated, the gist of all that the utmost research, among the musty tomes of the past, can furnish on the subject. This is followed by a statement, characterised by equal precision and completeness, of the doctrines of privilege now recognised, as belonging to legislative bodies, and, particularly, as guarantied by the Constitution of the United States to members of both Houses of Congress. He then answers the arguments of the counsel and apologists of the accused, consisting, mainly, of three propositions:

1. That the privilege claimed is undefined, and that the defence, and the mode of proceeding, and measure of punishment, ought to be defined by statute, before the House could take cognizance at all.

2. That the House has no power to arrest or imprison, except for some violence or disturbance in its presence, and that even in such case, it can only remove the offender, and prevent his return.

3. Or, if the House can take notice of a breach of privilege by assaulting a member for words spoken in debate, or for their publication, the offence must be committed while the member is in the actual performance of his duty, or is on his way *directly* to or from his lodgings and the hall of the House, or one of its committee rooms.

His reply to these propositions was brief, but unanswerable.

The defence had also contended that the House was an improper tribunal for the investigation of the offence charged, and had assigned nine specific reasons in support of that proposition.   Mr. Doddridge enumerated them, and refuted them in the order in which they had been stated, with irresistible effect; and yet this enumeration and refutation occupy only about a half page of his printed speech.

But those who desire to comprehend this great argument, must read it for themselves.   It must answer the present purpose, to present a few extracts from it, containing such general propositions as may serve as examples of the terse, lucid and incisive style of the speaker, and such as may be best understood and appreciated, without reference to the

context, although least essential to the conclusions he
aimed at.

"But, Mr. Speaker," said Mr. Doddridge, "there is a race of politicians so
wise in their own conceit, so self-sufficient, that they refuse to be instructed
by the opinions, or enlightened by the experience, of the whole world before
them—on whom the lights of history are shed in vain—a tribe of restless
men, who cannot be satisfied with the constructions of the race of statesmen
who made, and first administered the government of this country—to whom
it passes for nothing, if every Congress before the present exercised a given
power, or sustained a particular principle of construction. Yet these same
politicians are so vain, as to imagine that they, in the short life of their power,
can decide for all posterity. Thus it is, that, while now they are scattering
to the winds all precedents set before them in times ancient or modern, they
call upon us to be cautious of our doings, because we are now called on to decide the most important principle ever yet decided under the government,
and to decide it, too, for all posterity; forgetting that if their posterity shall
bear any resemblance to themselves, they will feel as little respect for their
opinions and principles, as they themselves possess for those of all the world
besides, past, present, or to come."

Again: "It has often been remarked, that the errors of wise men are apt
to be great and palpable, while those of weak men are but trivial. With
strong perceptions of truth, we seldom wander from the road of duty; but
when we do leave it, we do so by a course at right angles, never discovering
that we have left the King's highway, until we find ourselves entangled in
the thicket, or fast in a morass. With weaker minds and dim perceptions,
we stray oftener, diverging from our course, sometimes to the right, at others
to the left; we soon recover ourselves; yet when on the right path, we pursue
it but a short distance at a time, and even then, with feeble, trembling steps."

Referring to the importance of the principle involved in
the case—the freedom of debate—he said:

"I am sensible of the time misspent in the present investigation, and of
the importance of that time. But I am as sensible of the importance of the
principles involved in the decision we are about to make. We are about to
defend or surrender, the privileges, the rights, and even the liberties of our
constituents. These, and all that is dear to them, are at stake. In deciding
on the present question, this House will uphold the principles of our free

government, or permit its very foundation to be razed. For no one can believe that the representative principle can be maintained, when freedom of debate shall cease; without this, representation would be a vain thing. Whenever it shall happen that the representative of the people is restrained, by considerations of personal danger, from defending the rights and interests of those he represents, then representation ceases to exist but in name, and the government by whatever name it may be called, becomes arbitrary. There has been one common effort here, and out of doors, to arraign this House for attempting to secure to its members, exclusive privileges; the question has even been debated as if the privileges of the members of this House alone, and not those of the whole body of the people, were involved. This effort may be available to divert public opinion, for awhile, from the true question, but rely on it, that attention will soon be recalled."

Might not our ardent and impetuous modern reformers, social, political and moral, find a lesson worthy of their consideration, in the following terse and well-expressed sentences?

"In legislation, I hold it as an axiom, that laws must, in order to be wise, spring out of public opinion, and be conformable to it; and this, whether the lawgiver be a corporation sole, holding his power by birthright, or aggregate, and appointed by popular election. There is no profit in making and promulgating laws that cannot be executed; and laws, decidedly at war with popular opinion, cannot long be enforced. A legislator, if he is wise and experienced, may, in some degree, go beyond this; may improve, enlighten and control public opinion. That opinion, on the one hand, and the wisdom of the legislator on the other, may mutually act on each other as cause and effect; but essentially, wise legislation is but the expression of the popular will."

Those were times of high party excitement; and it had been more than intimated, on the floor of the House, as well as in the public journals of the country, that the President of the United States, if he did not instigate the assault made by Gen. Houston, at least, connived at it; and that the administration was not averse to the use of the bludgeon as a means of intimidating its political opponents in Congress.

Mr. Doddridge, in noticing this impeachment, true to his own self-respect, and to the sense of justice and generosity which always distinguished him, availed himself of the opportunity which the occasion afforded, to declare, that he had no authority for ascribing so unworthy a purpose either to the president or to his cabinet. But in the same connection, he animadverted with pointed severity upon a class of persons, not peculiar to that day, or to any age or country, or form of government, but found everywhere near the seat of power and patronage—hangers on—parasites—officious intermedlers, ready for any servile deed, by which they may hope to propitiate the favor, or minister to the passions of their patron—political pimps, eager to prostitute their own manhood by pandering to the lust of authority:

"I wish the House," said Mr. Doddridge, "to bear in mind, that, as I have no authority to ascribe the efforts against the constitution, and public liberty, of which I have been speaking, to the President, or to his past or present cabinet, so I do not charge or ascribe them. It is not a new thing in history, ancient or modern, for the friends of those already clothed with high powers, to offer to invest them with more—with absolute sway. Some there have been, whose patriotism compelled them to reject such offers. But, in the indulgence of unlimited confidence in him who is at the head of this government, there are those who would blindly break down all the safeguards, all the checks of the constitution, all barriers for the security of our liberties, in order to invest him with absolute power; little thinking of the shortness of the time during which he can hold it, or of the impossibility of preventing it from passing into other hands, or of restraining its exercise whenever it may fall into the hands of an ambitious President, disposed to respect no law but his own will, and to disregard all restraints on its free indulgence."

It was greatly to the credit and honor of the House of Representatives, that, notwithstanding the tremendous array of party influences in high and in low places,—by the public press, and by those clothed with official authority and patronage—brought to bear upon the case, the majority rose above all sinister and personal considerations, and by a decisive vote vindicated, what Charles James Fox, on a similar occasion, in the British Parliament, called "their privileges, their dignity, and their existence"—"The Code of Liberty." For this result, as was acknowledged at the time, the country was largely indebted to the powerful argument of Mr. Doddridge. On the 11th of May, 1832, the House, by a vote of 106 to 89, declared that "Samuel Houston has been guilty of a contempt and violation of the privileges of the House;" and thereupon, by the same vote, ordered that he be brought to the bar of the House and reprimanded by the Speaker for his said contempt and breach of privilege. This order was, accordingly, executed, on the 14th of May, 1832; and so terminated one of the most remarkable cases of the kind to be found in parliamentary history.

This speech gave Mr. Doddridge a national reputation. It attracted the attention, and received the high commendation of Mr. Webster. Mr. Madison read it, or had it read to him, in his retirement, and wrote of it: "Your speech is a very able one, as was to be expected"—endorsing its doctrines in the following words: "I have always considered the right of self-protection in the discharge of the necessary duties, as inherent in legislative bodies, as in courts of justice; in the State Legislatures, as in the British Parliament; and in the Federal Legislature as in both.*

At this time, the District of Columbia was without any regular code of laws. Until its retrocession to Virginia, that part of it lying south of the Potomac had remained

---

*Madison's writings, vol. 4, page 221.

subject to the laws of Virginia existing at the time of the original formation of the District; and that part of it lying north of the Potomac still remained subject to the laws of Maryland, as they were when the District was established; excepting as they had been modified by the occasional and irregular legislation of Congress. This evil had not, indeed, been remedied, so late as the year 1871. And it was even then a common saying among members of Congress, that there was no statutory law of the District of Columbia, respecting which there was absolute certainty, excepting an old statute of Maryland providing for the ducking of common scolds, which still remained unrepealed.

Mr. Doddridge, as a member of the House Committee on the District of Columbia, had greatly endeared himself to its people by his vigilant and considerate attention to their interests. As a testimonial of their high appreciation of his services, the authorities of the City of Washington caused an elegant portrait of him to be painted and placed in the City Hall. It might still have been seen there a few years ago—dusty and neglected. More recent inquiries after it, resulted in finding it stowed away at random among the old furniture and rubbish belonging to the corporation, without care, and, indeed, without recognition. Why not secure it to be brought home and hung up in the halls of the West Virginia Historical Society?

It was chiefly through his instrumentality that a special committee was appointed during this session of Congress, to draft a code of laws for the District, with leave to sit during the recess, before the next session. He was chairman of this committee. But instead of remaining together at the City of Washington, they apportioned their labors among themselves, and went home. Joseph M. White, the

Delegate from the Territory of Florida, was appointed
clerk of the committee, with instructions to remain in the
city.   It was arranged that each member of the committee
should prepare bills covering the portions of the code assigned to him, and send them to Mr. White, who should
make copies of them, and transmit one to each of the other
members of it; so that he should have time, prior to the
next session of Congress, to examine them and make such
notes of emendation as might suggest themselves as proper
to be made.   They were to meet at Washington two or
three weeks before Congress convened in December, 1832,
consolidate their separate work in proper order and form,
and so have their report of the entire code ready to be presented as soon as Congress assembled.   The portion of the
code allotted to Mr. Doddridge, was the Judiciary Department.   The writer of this paper was then a student reading
law in his office, and thus, had ample opportunity, so far as
he was able to appreciate them, to witness the industry and
ability which Mr. Doddridge brought to the discharge of
the important duty assigned to him.   The writer copied the
bills prepared by Mr. Doddridge to be sent to the clerk of
the committee; and, in this way, became familiar with the
mode which he pursued in preparing them.   It was this:
He had obtained the codes of several States.   When he
wished to prepare any particular chapter, he would read
the corresponding chapters in these codes, and then laying
them all aside, would, with wonderful rapidity, write off a
bill to suit himself.   It was, uniformly, much shorter than
that in any of the codes he consulted.   His facility as a
draftsman was remarkable.   He had a wonderful power of
condensation.   The appropriate words, like well-drilled
battalions, fell harmoniously into their proper places; and

there were neither too many, nor too few of them. It is
related of Mr. Webster, that he should have said, during a
tour he made through the Western States in 1833, whilst
stopping at Wheeling, that he would be willing to give all
he possessed if it would secure to him this extraordinary
faculty of Mr. Doddridge in the same degree of perfection.
The great Massachusetts statesman, often took occasion to
express his admiration of the abilities of Mr. Doddridge.
During the tour referred to, he stopped at Wellsburg, on
his way from Steubenville to Wheeling, for the express
purpose of paying his respects, personally, to Mrs. Doddridge.
Hearing that there was a portrait of Mr. Doddridge in the
town, he called to see it; and whilst he was looking at it,
remarked: "He was the only man I ever feared to meet in
debate." Nor was the impression which Mr. Doddridge
had made upon the mind of Mr. Webster of a transient
character. It remained indelible. In the letter of Mr.
Neeson, to which reference has already been made, is the
following: "During a recess of the Virginia Convention,
(1850–51), on my way from Marion county to Richmond,
I had the pleasure of spending an entire evening with Mr.
Webster, then Secretary of State, at Washington, at his
private office, in company with Judge Camden of Clarksburg, and Col. (afterwards General) Haymond, our representative in Congress. I well remember that Mr. Webster,
referring to the distinguished men of Virginia, spoke in
the kindest and most emphatic terms of the extraordinary
ability of Philip Doddridge. He indulged in eulogy of
Virginians, that evening, but his most exalted, was that
upon Philip Doddridge."

An incident may be appropriately mentioned here, shewing the power of Mr. Doddridge to concentrate the faculties

of his mind upon whatsoever engaged his attention, amount-
ing, almost, to complete abstraction from all else that surrounded him. While he was engaged upon the District
Code, in his office one day, his little daughter, some ten or
twelve years of age, came in, and with great glee and ani-
mation, announced to him, that his son "Biggs," whom he
had not seen for a long time, had come home from his residence in the West. His eye rested vacantly on the child,
and she, supposing that her message was understood, has-
tened away to her brother again. Mr. Doddridge was, in a
moment, absorbed in his work. In the course of half an
hour the same messenger returned, adding a request from
her mother, that her father should come to the house immediately. But still the father remained at his task. Half
an hour later, an elder daughter came in, and succeeded in
arousing him to a consciousness of the fact, when he has-
tened away with every manifestation of parental gratifica-
tion, to embrace his son.

According to the agreement already stated, Mr. Doddridge, having prepared the part of the code entrusted to
him, went on to the City of Washington several weeks before the assembling of Congress, to meet his colleagues on
the committee. He arrived there in due time; but he
never met the committee. After a brief illness, he expired
at Gadsby's Hotel, on the 19th of November, 1832; and
his honored remains now rest in the Congressional Cemetery, by the side of those of others of the country's public
servants, who died at the seat of government before the
modern facilities of transportation were invented. It was
noticeable, a few years ago, that the simple monuments
erected at their graves were becoming dilapidated, exhibit-
ing signs of neglect and decay. Would not West Virginia

perform a pious duty, and discharge a patriotic obligation by removing the remains of a citizen so eminent as was Mr. Doddridge, and re-interring them at some suitable place within her own borders?

His funeral obsequies, performed when Congress was not in session, attested the great respect with which he was regarded. The civic authorities of Washington, and many of the public functionaries of the United States government, united in them. Ex-President John Quincy Adams, who happened to be in the city, honored the ceremony with his presence; and the " *National Intelligencer*," distinguished for the dignity and propriety of its editorial department, and which always carefully measured its words of praise or censure, in announcing his decease, declared that in "intellectual ability and sound legal culture, he had scarcely a superior in the House." And when we remember, that such men as John Evans, of Maine, John Quincy Adams, Rufus Choate, and Edward Everett, of Massachusetts. Tristam Burges, of New Hampshire, Charles Fenton Mercer, of Virginia, George McDuffie, of South Carolina, and John Bell, and James K. Polk, of Tennessee, were then members of the House, this complimentary expression was equivalent to saying that Mr. Doddridge, in the respects mentioned, "had not a superior" in the whole nation. The corporate authorities of Alexandria passed a series of highly eulogistic resolutions expressing their sense of the loss the country had sustained in his demise.

On the first day of the second session of the twenty-first Congress, soon after the House of Representatives was called to order—

"Mr. Mercer rose and observed, That it was his melancholy duty to announce to the House the decease of his lamented colleague Philip Doddridge,

6

and to offer a resolution assuring the friends of the deceased, and the country at large, of the sense entertained by this House of the loss it has sustained. In performing this duty, Mr. Mercer said, that were he to indulge the feelings he possessed of the merits of his departed friend, he should find himself speedily arrested. In intellectual power that friend had been surpassed by few in this or any other country; in integrity of motive he was excelled by none; and in simplicity of heart, by no man he had ever known."

The resolution passed by the House, is as follows:

"*Resolved, unanimously,* That the members of the House of Representatives, from a sincere desire of shewing every mark of respect due to the memory of PHILIP DODDRIDGE, late a member thereof from the State of Virginia, will go into mourning by the usual mode of wearing crape around the left arm for one month."

On the fourth day of February, 1845, the Legislature of Virginia created a new county out of parts of Harrison, Lewis, Tyler and Ritchie counties; and following the praiseworthy custom of thus honoring the memory of the distinguished deceased citizens of the State, the name of DODDRIDGE was given to this new county. This was the first and only instance when the Legislature of Virginia ever bestowed such a distinction on a native or resident of Western Virginia—unless the Indian fighter, Lewis Wetzel, may be claimed as an exception. Famous Indians, male and female, have been thus honored; but the name of no citizen of the State west of the Alleghany Mountains, until that time, ever found such grace in the sight of the Legislature of Virginia—unless, indeed, Jackson county is another exception. Of the origin of the name of this county, the writer has no definite information.

ANALYTICAL.

A critical analysis of the character of Mr. Doddridge, will hardly be expected in a sketch like this. It may not, however, be out of place to refer to some of the more prominent traits which distinguished him. Among these, was his remarkable memory. Few men ever possessed this faculty in an equal degree. In his practice at the bar, he seldom made a written note of the testimony of the witnesses or of the arguments of counsel; yet neither of them were forgotten by him; and the one, and the other, were referred to, when necessary, with a readiness and accuracy, as if he were reading from a literal record of them. Nor was this accuracy of memory transient, or confined to recent proceedings. He could recall the evidence and arguments of cases which had occurred a quarter of a century before, with the freshness and particularity of the events of yesterday. The following will serve as an illustration of the tenacity of his memory: —

Some gentlemen were sitting with him in a hotel in Wellsburg in the summer of 1832. The yellow water-line made on the surrounding walls, by the extraordinary flood in the Ohio river in the month of February preceding, was

still visible. It seemed almost incredible, that the river
could ever have risen to such a height. Some one remarked
that it must have been a kind of Deucalion's flood. Immediately Mr. Doddridge seemed to be absorbed in thought.
After a few minutes, he clapped his hands, exclaiming—" I
have it—I have it;" and then repeated the whole of that
long, fine ode of Horace, commencing—

> " Jam satis terris, nivis atque diræ,
> "Grandinis misit, pater et rubente,
> " Dextera sacras jaculatus arces,
>   "Terruit urbem."

He declared that he had not seen, read or repeated it, since
he was a boy, forty years before.

It has been said, that where there is an extraordinary de-
velopment of the memory, the other mental faculties are
apt to be deficient. There have been remarkable instances
of this character. But there was no such defect in the
mental constitution of Mr. Doddridge. His judgment was
as sound, and discriminating, as his memory was compre-
hensive and exact. He had the clearest perception of the
relation of things: and his perception was as quick as it was
accurate. In the most complex cases at the bar, he promptly
comprehended the essential points; and such was his power
of classification, that the facts involved, however multifa-
rious, and the principles of law that were applicable, however abstruse or technical, instantly arranged themselves in
his mind with the most perfect logical precision. He saw,
at once, what was material, and immaterial, to the issue:
and he never burdened his argument, by minor or doubtful
propositions. But like the skilfull commander, divesting
himself, when going into action, of all unnecessary equip-
ments, which might impede the celerity of his movements,
or lessen the force of his attack, he did not encumber him-

self with the uncertain aid of secondary and trivial arguments, but relied on the clear, strong points of his case, and hurled them against the defences of his adversary with wonderful effect. He seldom spoke long; and before the Bench he had few equals; but before juries, he was not always so successful. They require more elaboration. Twelve undisciplined minds must be approached from different stand-points, before they are all effectively reached. The distinguishing power of Mr. Doddridge, consisted in the statement of a case, or a proposition, whether in the judicial or legislative forum. To do this well, is a great faculty; and it can belong only to great minds. When he had done this, as he usually did it, his argument was often complete; for the conclusions were patent and inevitable. The following is an example.

A case which excited great interest was pending in the United States Court at Columbus, Ohio. Henry Clay was retained as counsel on one side, and Mr. Doddridge on the other. The reputation of these distinguished advocates had attracted an immense concourse of people, both of ladies and gentlemen, to hear the discussion. It was a great public disappointment, that the former did not appear when the case was finally called for hearing; and the expectation was, thereupon, wholly concentrated on the latter. But when he arose, he merely read a few sentences from a slip of paper in his hand, stating the case, and then, with equal brevity, deduced the legal conclusions, and took his seat. Whilst the crowd was again disappointed, the Bench was filled with admiration. A complex and difficult controversy was reduced to a simple incontrovertible proposition: and the very words of Mr. Doddridge were afterwards incorporated in the final decision of the court.

It is sometimes the case, that where there is great breadth
of intellect, there is an incapacity to appreciate the value of
minor details.   There may be breadth without accuracy: a
large knowledge of general principles, without judgment to
restrict their application, in the business of life, by those
limitations which a prudent regard to actual surrounding
circumstances renders necessary.   In short, there are frequent instances of great knowledge, without corresponding
wisdom.   Men, possessing minds of this character, are apt
to be illogical, and unsafe counsellors.   But broad and com-
prehensive as was the mind of Mr. Doddridge, it was also
eminently practical.   It would be difficult to find a more
exact and conclusive reasoner than he was.   His arguments,
brief, clear and axiomatic, often resembled, in their precision and compactness, the demonstration of a proposition in
Euclid.

It is sometimes said that there is a tendency in the pursuits of the barrister to narrow the mind, and render it more
technical than profound; that lawyers are seldom reformers:
that hampered by precedents, subservient to authorities,
and restrained by the habits of their profession, from original investigations, they seldom rise above the wisdom of the
past into new and higher spheres of thought and progress.
There may be a tendency in the study and practice of the
law, to inspire conservatism.   Mr. Doddridge was conspic-
uously conservative in his character.   But whilst he rever-
enced "the fathers," and, sometimes, sharply rebuked those
reckless innovators, who are ever ready to rush into untried
paths, regardless of the experience and teachings of those
who have traveled before them, he was not averse to change
and to progress.   Nay, he sought and challenged them, on
proper occasions, as his course in the Virginia Convention

amply demonstrates. His reply there, to the opponents of
constitutional reform, who were constantly warning him
against the dangers of revolution and anarchy, for terseness
and vigor of style, clearness of historical facts, within limited compass, is hardly exceeded by the finest passage of
Tacitus. Witness the following extract:

"But the ball of revolution, once set in motion, rolls down to anarchy first,
and then to despotism! It never returns! And is this really so? Permit
me to call the attention of the committee to some of the civil revolutions of
England, (for there have been several), in which the ball of revolution *as-
cended,* and stopped at the point desired; and the fruits of which are now the
boast, both of that country, and of this. On what does the Englishman pride
himself, when contrasting his condition with that of the subject of any other
country? The answer readily occurs: the great and lesser charter of English
liberties; jury trial, the *habeas corpus,* the common law, the right of suffrage;
in short, the Englishman rejoices in his civil and religious liberties; in a government of laws. Among all his blessings, he is in the habit of naming
magna charta as the first; when and how was that charter obtained? It was
obtained by *revolution* at Runny Meade. A majority of the Barons demanded
of King John a charter of privileges and liberties, as English subjects. The
King refused; and this majority of Barons armed themselves (for *numbers*
ruled there). The King wrote to them to know, what were these liberties
and privileges about which they were so anxious. The Barons answered,
that the privileges they demanded were granted by the King's father. From
this answer it is supposed that the great charter had been granted by King
Henry the Third. This fact is not certain, however, nor is it important: the
King signed certain articles of agreement, promising a charter of the rights
demanded, which the Barons had drawn up in writing, as we propose to do:
he engaged to meet them on a certain day, in July, 1215, to give full effect to
this agreement. Instead of performing what he promised to do in good faith,
the King interposed a difficulty; that difficulty was not of freemen and vil-
lains, of men and taxes, or of federal numbers. He wrote to the Pope, and
placed his kingdom under his protection, offering himself for a crusade to the
Holy Land, and when the day arrived, instead of performing his engagement,
he informed the Barons of his intentions, and that his kingdom being now
the patrimony of St. Peter, they could not touch it without impious (if I re-
collect we have heard this word here) hands. The Barons, on receipt of this

evasive answer, attacked and carried several of the King's castles; and, as
the Pope could give no assistance, and St. Peter came not to claim his heri-
tage, the King and his *minority* had to yield to a *majority* of Barons. The
charter was signed and sealed, and with the agreement which preceded it, is
preserved in the tower of London to this day. This charter is a body of what
we would now call common law—of family law.

"This glorious civil revolution was effected in two or three short months
in the year 1215. Between that year and the year 1688 several revolutions
occurred, and were attended with the same happy results, the consequences
of which were frequent renewals of the great, and the additions of the lesser
charter, and the *articuli super cartas.* In each of these revolutions the ball
was rolled up, and at the end of each, the rights of the people who rolled it,
acquired additional strength.

"I pass on to the well known revolution of 1688. Until this time England had never known the blessings of an independent judiciary. The
tenure *quam diu bene se gesserit,* had never been inserted but in one commis-
sion. Great as was the value placed by our Whig ancestors in 1688, on their
charters, their laws, their jury trial, and their writ of *habeas corpus,* they
looked upon their rights and privileges as in some degree of danger, so long
as the judges were dependent on the King or his ministry. The gentleman
from Chesterfield said the other day, that when the King is weak and profli-
gate, the rights of the people gain ground. William was weak at least; his
ruling desire was to insert in the act of settlement, a provision limiting the
succession to the heirs of his kins-woman, the Princess Sophia, of Hanover :
he was too weak to perceive that his parliament were determined to do this
at all events; that no other course could consist with their policy. The parliament practiced on the King's weakness, and as a consideration for the settlement of the crown, extorted his concession that the Judges of England
should hold their commissions *during good behavior.* Unfortunately for
Scotland and Ireland, this provision was omitted in each of their acts of
union with England, and the effects of judicial dependence and independence have been manifested in the three kingdoms in our own days. A great
effort, common to the Whigs of England, Ireland and Scotland, was made
at the same time. The object was parliamentary reform. The necessity of
reform was manifest. The means proposed were orderly and constitutional.
Government endeavored to suppress the United Irish in Ireland, the friends
of reform in Scotland, and corresponding societies in London. In conflicts
between government and people, considerable excess happened in each king-

dom. The laws of Ireland differed from those of Scotland, and the laws of each from those of England; I mean those relating to crimes and punishments; the greatest difference was in the Forums, before which the subjects of each kingdom were brought for trial. The Englishman was brought before independent judges; those of Ireland and Scotland before judges amenable to the King and his ministers. The Irishman suffered death; the Scotchman banishment; while the Englishman was acquitted and greeted as a patriot. Englishmen were not yet satisfied with the concession of William; the judges were not secure from a demise of the crown, and this defect, at length, was remedied by the statute in the reign of one of the Georges. Here is a brief history of four or five civil revolutions, if our present effort may be called one. All these happened in our mother country. Before the first, the government of that country was a feudal monarchy—a despotism; since the last, it is a free-limited monarchy. These civil revolutions have made that government such, that it is receiving every day the warm and reiterated plaudits of our opponents on this floor. From the last of these revolutions, we have copied our independent judiciary; and, although I will aid to create more responsibility there, I pray that we and our posterity to remotest time, may never be weak enough to part with this surest, greatest sheet anchor of every free State."

Mr. Doddridge was not a learned man—if extensive literary and scientific acquirements are to be included in the meaning of that term. He was a select, rather than miscellaneous, or extended reader; but what he read, he read well—storing away whatever was valuable in the treasury of his never-failing memory,—not in chaotic confusion, as some men gluttonously devour knowledge, but well digested, classified and in order, ready for appropriation whenever there was a demand for it. He was, however, most thoroughly conversant with the legal, political, and constitutional history of Great Britain, and of his own country.

Nor was he, what is called, "a case lawyer." Although familiar with a wide range of reported cases, and, especially with those of Virginia, and of the Supreme court of the United States, he did not often elaborately refer to them in his arguments. When he did cite a case, however, it was sure to be very much to the point, and to cover, completely, the question involved. His knowledge of the elementary principles of legal science was so thorough, and his power of enunciating them clearly, so extraordinary, that he seldom needed the authority of adjudicated cases to support his positions. He, usually, reversed the order of that class of lawyers who ransack all the reports in their library to find a principle; he announced the principle at once, assured that those who deemed it necessary to search for them, would find the decisions sustaining it.

A gentleman well acquainted with him in the prime of his life, and eminently qualified to form an intelligent opinion of such a matter, writes: "Mr. Doddridge was not great (great as he was) from education, or early associations, but from natural endowment. If he had had the education and associations of Webster, he would, undoubtedly in public estimation and in fact, have been his compeer, if not his superior. Perhaps it was, in some measure, owing to the comparatively limited range of his scientific and literary researches that he was enabled to concentrate his great powers in the study of law, and thus become the great elementary lawyer that he was. I remember once, at a private dinner party in Richmond, when Mr. Doddridge, incidentally, became the subject of remark, hearing Chief Justice Marshall say, that Doddridge, as a lawyer, was second to no one at the Bar of the United States Court." *

---

*Extract from a letter of John C. Campbell, Esq., of Ohio county, West Virginia. Nor was this gentleman's estimate of Mr. Doddridge as a statesman less appreciative. In a letter written to the author, from Richmond, shortly after the death of Mr. Doddridge, he says: "The loss of our distinguished friend, Philip Doddridge, at any time, would have been, to the public, a great misfortune, but at the present crisis it is a national calamity. His talents, firmness, and political integrity, turned the eyes of all wise and patriotic statesmen to him, as one, amongst a few others, who were expected to breast the coming storm."

Another distinguishing feature in the character of Mr. Doddridge, was his ingenuousness. He abhored all shams. At the bar, he scorned the chicanery and trickery of the pettifogger. On the hustings, as well as in the halls of the legislative assembly, he never stooped to the arts of the demagogue. His intellect was too large to form an alliance with anything so paltry. But, as not unfrequently happens to great natures, he was sometimes the dupe of the designing, and the victim of misplaced confidence. Conscious of his own candor, he was slow to suspect others of duplicity. It may be said of him, as Macauley said of his friend Lord Holland, that he possessed a "magnanimous credulity of mind, which was as incapable of suspecting as of devising mischief."

It is one of the recognized canons of literary criticism, that simplicity is essential in the sublime. Sad experience has taught us, that we may not always rigidly apply the same test in our judgment of *great minds;* for, whilst it was said of Bacon that he was "the greatest," it had also to be said, that he was "the meanest of mankind." Yet simplicity is essential to the perfection of all truly great *characters;* and such simplicity, without "guile or hypocrisy," Mr. Doddridge did possess in an eminent degree. It was no unmeaning compliment of Mr. Mercer, when he declared in the United States House of Representatives, that "In simplicity of heart Mr. Doddridge was excelled by no man he had ever seen."

It could not be said, in the ordinary sense of the word, that he was an orator. But he possessed, in an eminent degree, the qualities of a good speaker. His articulation, although a little guttural, was distinct; his language was pure and exact; his style was chaste and perspicuous; his utterance was easy and unhesitating; and his manner, though not rhetorical, was emphatic and forcible. He addressed himself to the understanding, more than to the imagination; and the weight of his arguments was never impaired by the embellishment of fancy.

His manners were simple and unostentatious. He was the charm of the social circle. His conversation flowed as a perennial fountain, sparkling with a genial wit, and redolent of the kindness and goodness of his heart. With a memory stored with the treasures of history, and rich in anecdotes and personal incidents, he had the happiest facility in relating them; and was the centre of attraction and delight, in whatsoever society he was placed.

Mr. Doddridge possessed the faculty of intuition, in a remarkable degree. In the investigation of cases at the bar, he seemed to comprehend them, oftentimes, long before all the facts were disclosed by the evidence. His great experience, doubtless, qualified him, in a measure, to do this; but aside from this, he had an extraordinary penetration, that anticipated what was to come with almost unerring certainty. He frequently surprised witnesses by telling them what they knew, before they had fully stated it; and such as were disposed to prevaricate, or to falsify, seldom escaped from his examination without being exposed and confounded. He often cut short the prolix stories of his clients, in making known their cases, by giving the particulars of them himself. The following is an illustrative instance:—

A gentleman called to consult him on professional business, and had partially related the matters involved, when Mr. Doddridge interposed, and briefly, but succinctly, detailed the remaining facts with such exactness as greatly to surprise his client, who inquired of him, from whom he had received his information. "From no person," said Mr. Doddridge; "but from what you have told me, I know the facts must be as I have stated them."

A correspondent* furnishes the following incident, upon the authority of Jesse Edgington, Esq., who was a cotemporary and worthy associate of Mr. Doddridge, and who lived to an extreme old age, dying only a few years ago, revered and respected by all who knew him. It affords an illustration of the charm and versatility of Mr. Doddridge's conversational powers, as well as of his retentive memory, and of the faculty of analysis and intuition just referred to.

"They were traveling on horseback to Richmond, and, in Maryland, were joined by a Mr. Hayden, of Chambersburg, Pennsylvania. That charming romance, Guy Mannering, had just been published in this country, but had not reached the West. Mr. Hayden had read it, and in whiling away the hours of the long ride, gave a pretty thorough sketch of it. After their arrival at Richmond, they met at a dinner party, and Guy Mannering being the subject of conversation, Mr. Doddridge gave such a clear and graphic resume of it as enchanted his auditors — making Meg Merrilies, Dandy Dinmont, Pleydell, and others, stand out in perfect relief in their true characters before them. Hayden was astonished; rather indignant, indeed, and took the first opportunity, privately, to say to Mr. Doddridge: 'Sir, I thought you said that you had not read that book?' 'Nor have I,' replied Mr. Doddridge; 'all I know about it is what you told me.'"

Mr. Doddridge was a regular attendant upon the ministry and services of the Protestant Episcopal Church; but whether he was a communicant, is not now remembered by the writer. He had, however, a solemn regard for the word of God, and the greatest reverence for Christianity. Any levity respecting either, especially on the part of the young, was sure to evoke some manifestation of his displeasure. Can there be true greatness without this religious

*James E. Wharton, Esq., Mansfield, Ohio.

element of character? Young men, animated by a true
ambition, should ponder well this question. Mr. Webster,
in pronouncing a public eulogium on that great lawyer, Mr.
Jeremiah Mason, of Boston, said:

"Nothing of character is really permanent but virtue and personal worth.
These remain. Whatever of excellence is wrought in the soul itself belongs
to both worlds. Real goodness does not attach itself merely to this life; it
points to another world. Political or professional reputation cannot last forever; but a conscience void of offence before God and man is an inheritance
for eternity. Religion, therefore, is a necessary and indispensable element in
any great human character. There is no living without it. Religion is the
tie that connects man with his Creator, and holds him to His throne. If that
tie be all sundered, all broken, he floats away, a worthless atom in the uni-
verse; its proper attractions all gone, its destiny thwarted, and its whole future nothing but darkness, desolation and death. A man with no sense of
religious duty is he whom the scriptures describe, in terse and terrific language, as living 'without God in the world.' Such a man is out of his proper
being, out of the circle of all his duties, out of the circle of all his happiness,
and away, far, far away, from the purpose of his creation."

Mr. Doddridge never appeared to greater advantage, than
at home surrounded by his family. Great minds, and especially great students, are, sometimes, deficient in those
social characteristics which give the chief charm to the do-
mestic relations. They become married, as it were, to their
books, and retire to the seclusion of their libraries. Absorbed in their studies, or engrossed with their professional
pursuits, they have no relish for the amenities and fellow-
ship of the family circle; and the affections of the husband
and parent lie dormant and undeveloped. It was not so
with Mr. Doddridge. Simple, unassuming, genial, and
gentle everywhere, his presence at home was always hailed
with delight by his children, old and young, who clustered
about him in the unreserved confidence of mutual pleasure
and affection, and the reciprocity of kind offices.

Mr. Doddridge died in the maturity and full vigor of his wonderful intellect, just at the time when his eminent abilities and distinction in the chief council-chamber of the nation, had so attracted and commanded the public attention and confidence, as to presage for him a higher, and still more illustrious career. More than forty-two years have, in vain, awaited a competent biographer. Until there shall appear a pen more worthy of the sacred task, this imperfect sketch is here recorded by one who has reason to cherish his memory.

A SUGGESTION.

On the second day of July, 1864, the Congress of the United States passed a resolution inviting the several States to furnish "two full-length marble statues of deceased persons, who have been citizens thereof, and illustrious for their renown, or from civic or military services, such as each State shall determine to be worthy of national commemoration," to be placed in the old Hall of the House of Representatives.

Some of the States have, already, responded to this invitation. Rhode Island has furnished statues of General Nathaniel Greene and Roger Williams; and Connecticut, those of Jonathan Trumbull and Roger Sherman. Other States, doubtless, will avail themselves of the same grateful privilege. It is, respectfully, suggested, that West Virginia shall follow this patriotic example. She cannot hesitate as to the first person to be thus honored; and in placing the statue of Philip Doddridge among those of the illustrious sons of the Republic, she will have the proud satisfaction of knowing, that she has done all that the marble image of one of her own sons can do, to perpetuate the name and memory of one of the greatest minds that ever adorned the nation.

A SKETCH

OF

THE LIFE

OF

PHILIP DODDRIDGE.

BY

W. T. WILLEY.

READ BEFORE THE WEST VIRGINIA HISTORICAL SOCIETY,
AT ITS ANNUAL MEETING HELD IN THE
WEST VIRGINIA UNIVERSITY,
JUNE, 1875.

PUBLISHED BY ORDER OF THE SOCIETY

MORGANTOWN
MORGAN & HOFFMAN, PRINTERS.
1875.

www.ingramcontent.com/pod-product-compliance
Lightning Source LLC
Chambersburg PA
CBHW032356280326
41935CB00008B/600